SMITH
WIGGLESWORTH
On
Spirit-Filled
Living

Other Whitaker House Titles
by Smith Wigglesworth

SMITH
WIGGLESWORTH
On
Spirit-Filled
Living

Smith Wigglesworth

W

WHITAKER
HOUSE

Whitaker House gratefully acknowledges and thanks Glenn Gohr and the entire staff of the Assemblies of God Archives in Springfield, Missouri, for graciously assisting us in compiling Smith Wigglesworth's works for publication in this book.

All Scripture quotations are taken from the *New King James Version* (NKJV), © 1979, 1980, 1982, 1984 by Thomas Nelson, Inc. Used by permission. All rights reserved.

Publisher's note: This new edition from Whitaker House has been updated for the modern reader. Words, expressions, and sentence structure have been revised for clarity and readability. Although the more modern Bible translation quoted in this edition was not available to Smith Wigglesworth, it was carefully and prayerfully selected in order to make the language of the entire text readily understandable while maintaining his original premises and message.

SMITH WIGGLESWORTH ON SPIRIT-FILLED LIVING

ISBN: 0-88368-534-5
Printed in the United States of America
© 1998 by Whitaker House

Whitaker House
1030 Hunt Valley Circle
New Kensington, PA 15068
www.whitakerhouse.com

Library of Congress Cataloging-in-Publication Data

Wigglesworth, Smith, 1859–1947.
Smith Wigglesworth on Spirit-filled living / by Smith Wigglesworth.
p.   cm.
ISBN 0-88368-534-5 (trade paper : alk. paper)
1. Pentecostal churches—Sermons. 2. Spiritual life—Pentecostal authors—Sermons. 3. Sermons, English. I. Title.
BX8762.Z6W56   1998
252' .0994—dc21   98-17192

---

5 6 7 8 9 10 11 12 13 14 ▮▮▮ 12 11 10 09 08 07 06 05 04

Contents

Introduction

An encounter with Smith Wigglesworth was an unforgettable experience. This seems to be the universal reaction of all who knew him or heard him speak. Smith Wigglesworth was a simple yet remarkable man who was used in an extraordinary way by our extraordinary God. He had a contagious and inspiring faith. Under his ministry, thousands of people came to salvation, committed themselves to a deeper faith in Christ, received the baptism in the Holy Spirit, and were miraculously healed. The power that brought these kinds of results was the presence of the Holy Spirit, who filled Smith Wigglesworth and used him in bringing the good news of the Gospel to people all over the world. Wigglesworth gave glory to God for everything that was accomplished through his ministry, and he wanted people to understand his work only in this context, because his sole desire was that people would see Jesus and not himself.

Smith Wigglesworth was born in England in 1859. Immediately after his conversion as a boy, he had a concern for the salvation of others and won people to Christ, including his mother. Even so, as a young man, he could not express himself well enough to give a testimony in church, much less preach a sermon. Wigglesworth said that his mother had the same difficulty in expressing herself that he did. This family trait, coupled with the fact that he had no formal education because he began working twelve hours a day at the age of seven to help support the family, contributed to Wigglesworth's awkward speaking style. He became a plumber by trade, yet he continued to devote himself to winning many people to Christ on an individual basis.

In 1882, he married Polly Featherstone, a vivacious young woman who loved God and had a gift of preaching and evangelism. It was she who taught him to read and who became his closest confidant and strongest supporter. They both had compassion for the poor and needy in their community, and they opened a mission, at which Polly preached. Significantly, people were miraculously healed when Wigglesworth prayed for them.

In 1907, Wigglesworth's circumstances changed dramatically when, at the age of forty-eight, he was baptized in the Holy Spirit. Suddenly, he had a new power that enabled him to preach, and even his wife was amazed at the transformation. This was the beginning of what became a worldwide evangelistic and healing ministry that reached thousands. He eventually ministered in the United States, Australia, South Africa, and all over Europe. His ministry extended up to the time of his death in 1947.

Several emphases in Smith Wigglesworth's life and ministry characterize him: a genuine, deep compassion for the unsaved and sick; an unflinching belief in the Word of God; a desire that Christ should increase and he should decrease (John 3:30); a belief that he was called to exhort people to enlarge their faith and trust in God; an emphasis on the baptism in the Holy Spirit with the manifestation of the gifts of the Spirit as in the early church; and a belief in complete healing for everyone of all sickness.

Smith Wigglesworth was called "The Apostle of Faith" because absolute trust in God was a constant theme of both his life and his messages. In his meetings, he would quote passages from the Word of God and lead lively singing to help build people's faith and encourage them to act on it. He emphasized belief in the fact that God could do the impossible. He had great faith in what God could do, and God did great things through him.

Wigglesworth's unorthodox methods were often questioned. As a person, Wigglesworth was reportedly courteous, kind, and gentle. However, he became forceful when dealing with the Devil, whom he believed caused all sickness. Wigglesworth said the reason he spoke bluntly and acted forcefully with people was that he knew he needed to get their attention so they could focus on God. He also had such anger toward the Devil and sickness that he acted in a seemingly rough way. When he prayed for people to be healed, he would often hit or punch them at the place of their problem or illness. Yet, no one was hurt by this startling treatment. Instead, they were remarkably healed. When he was asked why he treated people in this manner, he said that he was not hitting the people but that he was hitting the Devil. He believed that Satan should never be treated gently or allowed to get away with anything. About twenty people were reportedly raised from the dead after he prayed for them. Wigglesworth himself was healed of appendicitis and kidney stones, after which his personality softened and he was more gentle with those who came to him for prayer for healing. His abrupt manner in ministering may be attributed to the fact that he was very serious about his calling and got down to business quickly.

Although Wigglesworth believed in complete healing, he encountered illnesses and deaths that were difficult to understand. These included the deaths of his wife and son, his daughter's lifelong deafness, and his own battles with kidney stones and sciatica.

He often seemed paradoxical: compassionate but forceful, blunt but gentle, a well-dressed gentleman whose speech was often ungrammatical or confusing. However, he loved God with everything he had, he was steadfastly committed to God and to His Word, and he didn't rest until he saw God move in the lives of those who needed Him.

In 1936, Smith Wigglesworth prophesied about what we now know as the charismatic movement. He accurately predicted that the established mainline denominations would experience revival and the gifts of the Spirit in a way that would surpass even the Pentecostal movement. Wigglesworth did not live to see the renewal, but as an evangelist and prophet with a remarkable healing ministry, he had a tremendous influence on both the Pentecostal and charismatic movements, and his example and influence on believers is felt to this day.

Without the power of God that was so obviously present in his life and ministry, we might not be reading transcripts of his sermons, for his spoken messages were often disjointed and ungrammatical. However, true gems of spiritual insight shine through them because of the revelation he received

Introduction

through the Holy Spirit. It was his life of complete devotion and belief in God and his reliance on the Holy Spirit that brought the life-changing power of God into his messages.

As you read this book, it is important to remember that Wigglesworth's works span a period of several decades, from the early 1900s to the 1940s. They were originally presented as spoken rather than written messages, and necessarily retain some of the flavor of a church service or prayer meeting. Some of the messages were Bible studies that Wigglesworth led at various conferences. At his meetings, he would often speak in tongues and give the interpretation, and these messages have been included as well. Because of Wigglesworth's unique style, the sermons and Bible studies in this book have been edited for clarity, and archaic expressions that would be unfamiliar to modern readers have been updated.

In conclusion, we hope that as you read these words of Smith Wigglesworth, you will truly sense his complete trust and unwavering faith in God and take to heart one of his favorite sayings: "Only believe!"

1

Extraordinary

The people in whom God delights are the ones who rest upon His Word without doubting. God has nothing for the man who wavers, *"for let not that man suppose that he will receive anything from the Lord"* (James 1:7). Therefore, I would like us to get this verse deep into our hearts until it penetrates every fiber of our being:

> Only believe, only believe.
> All things are possible; only believe.

God has a plan beyond anything that we have ever known. He has a plan for every individual life, and if we have any other plan in view, we miss the grandest plan of all. Nothing in the past is equal to the present, and nothing in the present can equal the things of tomorrow. Tomorrow should be so filled with holy expectations that we will be living flames for Him. God never intended His people to be ordinary or commonplace. His intentions were that they should be on fire for Him, conscious of His divine power, realizing the glory of the Cross that foreshadows the crown.

SANCTIFIED UNTO GOD

God has given us a very special Scripture:

Now in those days, when the number of the disciples was multiplying, there arose a complaint against the Hebrews by the Hellenists, because their widows were neglected in the daily distribution. Then the twelve summoned the multitude of the disciples and said, "It is not desirable that we should leave the word of God and serve tables. Therefore, brethren, seek out from among you seven men of good reputation, full of the Holy Spirit and wisdom, whom we may appoint over this business...." And the saying pleased the whole multitude. And they chose Stephen, a man full of faith and the Holy Spirit, and Philip. (Acts 6:1–3, 5)

During the time of the inauguration of the church, the disciples were pressured by many responsibilities. The practical things of life could not be attended to, and many were complaining concerning the neglect of their widows. Therefore, the disciples decided upon a plan, which was to choose seven men to do the work of caring for the needs of these widows—men who were *"full of the Holy Spirit."* What a divine thought. No matter what kind of work was to be done, however menial it may have been, the person chosen had to be *"full of the Holy Spirit."* The plan of the church was that everything, even everyday routines, must be sanctified to God, for the church had to be a Holy Spirit church. Beloved, God has never ordained anything less.

Extraordinary

ENDUED WITH POWER

I want to stress one thing. First and foremost, I would emphasize these questions: Have you received the Holy Spirit since you believed? Are you filled with divine power?

The heritage of the church is to be so equipped with power that God can lay His hand upon any member at any time to do His perfect will. There is no stopping point in the Spirit-filled life. We begin at the Cross, the place of disgrace, shame, and death, and that very death brings the power of resurrection life. Then, being filled with the Holy Spirit, we go on *"from glory to glory"* (2 Cor. 3:18). Let us not forget that possessing the baptism in the Holy Spirit means that there must be an ever increasing holiness. How the church needs divine anointing. It needs to see God's presence and power so evidenced that the world will recognize it. People know when the tide is flowing; they also know when it is ebbing.

The necessity for seven men to be chosen for the position of serving tables was very evident. The disciples knew that these seven men were men ready for active service, and so they chose them. In Acts 6:5, we read: *"And the saying pleased the whole multitude. And they chose Stephen, a man full of faith and the Holy Spirit, and Philip."*

There were others, but Stephen and Philip stand out most prominently in the Scriptures. Philip was a man so filled with the Holy Spirit that a revival always followed wherever he went. Stephen was a man so filled with divine power that although serving tables might have been all right in the minds of the other disciples, God had a greater vision for him. God filled him with a baptism of fire, with power and divine anointing, that took him on to the climax of his life when he saw right into the open heavens (Acts 7:56).

Had we been there with the disciples at that time, I believe we would have heard them saying to each other, "Look here. Neither Stephen nor Philip are doing the work we called them to. If they do not attend to business, we will have to get someone else." That is the human way of thinking, but divine order is far above our finite planning. When we please God in our daily service, we will always find that everyone who is faithful in the little things, God will make ruler over much (Matt. 25:21).

Stephen is such an example to follow. He was a man chosen to serve tables, who had such a revelation of the mind of Christ and of the depth and height of God that there was no standing still in his experience. He went forward with leaps and bounds. Beloved, there is a race to be run, a crown to be won. We cannot stand still. I say to you, be vigilant. Be vigilant. Let no one *"take your crown"* (Rev. 3:11).

ABOVE THE ORDINARY

God has privileged us in Christ Jesus to live above the ordinary human plane of life. Those who want to be ordinary and live on a lower plane can do so, but as for me, I will not. The same unction, the same zeal, the same Holy Spirit power is at our command as it was at the command of Stephen and the apostles. We have the same God that Abraham and Elijah had, and we do not need to lag behind in receiving any gift or grace. We may not possess all the gifts as abiding gifts, but as we are full of the Holy Spirit and divine unction, it is possible, when there is a need, for God to make evident every gift of the Spirit through us as He may choose to use.

Stephen, an ordinary man, became extraordinary under the Holy Spirit's anointing until, in many ways, he stands supreme among the apostles. *"And Stephen, full of faith and power, did great wonders and signs among the people"* (Acts 6:8). As we go deeper in God, He enlarges our capacity for understanding and places before us a wide-open door. I am not surprised that this man chosen to serve tables was afterwards called to a higher plane.

You may ask, "What do you mean? Did he stop taking care of his responsibilities?" No, but he was lost in the power of God. He lost sight of everything in the natural and steadfastly fixed his gaze upon Jesus, *"the author and finisher of our faith"* (Heb. 12:2), until he was transformed into a shining light in the kingdom of God. May we be awakened to believe His Word and to understand the mind of the Spirit, for there is an inner place of purity where we can see God. Stephen was just as ordinary a person as you and I, but he was in the place where God could move him so that he, in turn, could affect those around him. He began in a humble place and ended in a blaze of glory. Dare to believe Christ.

FACING THE OPPOSITION

As you go on in this life of the Spirit, you will find that the Devil will begin to get restless and will cause a dispute in the church; it was so with Stephen. Any number of people may be found in the church who are very proper in a worldly sense—

always correctly dressed, the elite of the city, welcoming everything into the church but the power of God. Let us read what God says about them:

> *Then there arose some from what is called the Synagogue of the Freedmen (Cyrenians, Alexandrians, and those from Cilicia and Asia), disputing with Stephen. And they were not able to resist the wisdom and the Spirit by which he spoke.* (Acts 6:9–10)

The Freedmen, or Libertines, could not stand the truth of God. With these opponents, Stephen found himself in the same predicament as the blind man whom Jesus healed. As soon as the blind man's eyes were opened, the Pharisees threw him out of the synagogue. (See John 9:1–38.) They did not want anybody in the synagogue who had his eyes open. As soon as you receive spiritual eyesight, out you go! These Freedmen, Cyrenians, and Alexandrians rose up full of wrath in the very place where they should have been full of the power of God, full of love divine, and full of reverence for the Holy Spirit. They rose up against Stephen, this man *"full of the Holy Spirit"* (Acts 6:3).

Beloved, if there is anything in your life that in any way resists the power of the Holy Spirit and the entrance of His Word into your heart and life, drop on your knees and cry aloud for mercy. When the Spirit of God is waiting at your heart's door, do not resist Him; instead, open your heart to the touch of God. Resistance is good if it is applied to fighting evil. For instance, there is a resisting to the point of *"bloodshed, striving against sin"* (Heb. 12:4), but resisting the Holy Spirit (Acts 7:51) will drive you into sin.

MIGHTY FOR GOD

Stephen spoke with remarkable wisdom, and things began to happen. You will find that there is always a moving when the Holy Spirit has control. Brought under conviction by the message of Stephen, his opponents resisted, they lied, they did anything and everything to stifle that conviction. Not only did they lie, but they got others to lie against Stephen, who would have laid down his life for any one of them. Stephen was used by God to heal the sick, perform miracles, and yet they brought false accusations against him (Acts 6:13–14). What effect did these false charges have on Stephen? *"And all who sat in the council, looking stedfastly at him, saw his face as the face of an angel"* (v. 15).

Something had happened in the life of this man. Chosen for menial service, he became mighty for God. How was it accomplished in him? It was because his aim was high. Stephen was faithful in little, and God brought him to full fruition. Under the inspiration of divine power by which he spoke, the council could not help but listen to his holy, prophetic words. Beginning with Abraham and Moses, Stephen continued unfolding the truth. What a marvelous exhortation! Take your Bible and read it. Listen in as the angels listened in. As light upon light, truth upon truth, revelation upon revelation, found its way into their hearts, they gazed at him in astonishment. Their hearts perhaps became warm at times, and they may have said, "Truly, this man is sent by God"—but then he hurled the truth at them:

> *You stiffnecked and uncircumcised in heart and ears! You always resist the Holy Spirit; as your fathers did, so do you. Which of the prophets did your fathers not persecute? And they killed those who foretold the coming of the Just One, of whom you now have become the betrayers and murderers, who have received the law by the direction of angels and have not kept it.* (Acts 7:51–53)

Then what happened? These men were moved; they were *"cut to the heart, and they gnashed at him with their teeth"* (v. 54).

There are two occasions in the Scriptures where people were *"cut to the heart."* After Peter had delivered that inspired sermon on the Day of Pentecost, the people were *"cut to the heart"* (Acts 2:37) with conviction, and there were added to the church 3,000 souls (v. 41). Here is Stephen, speaking under the inspiration of the Holy Spirit, and the men of this council who were being *"cut to the heart"* rose up as one man to slay him. As you read Acts 7, beginning with verse fifty-five, what a picture you have before you. As I close my eyes, I have a vision of this scene in every detail: the howling mob with their vengeful, murderous spirits, ready to devour this holy man, and he *"being full of the Holy Spirit, gazed into heaven and saw the glory of God."* What did he see there? From his place of helplessness, he looked up and said: *"I see the heavens opened and the Son of Man standing at the right hand of God!"* (v. 56).

Is that the position that Jesus left earth to take? No. He went to *sit* at the right hand of the Father (Heb. 12:2); but in support of the first martyr, in behalf of the man with that burning flame of Holy Spirit power, God's Son *stood up* in honorary testimony of him who, called to serve tables, was faithful unto death.

But is that all? No, I am so glad that is not all. As the stones came flying at Stephen, pounding his body, crushing his bones, striking his temple, mangling his beautiful face, what happened? How did this scene end? With a sublime, upward look, this man, chosen for an ordinary task but filled with the Holy Spirit, was so moved upon by God that he finished his earthly work in a blaze of glory, magnifying God with his last breath. Looking up into the face of the Master, he said, *"'Lord, do not charge them with this sin.' And when he had said this, he fell asleep"* (Acts 7:60).

Friends, it is worth everything to gain the Holy Spirit. What a divine ending to the life and testimony of a man who was chosen to serve tables.

2

Divine Revelation

raise the Lord. Praise the Lord. "Only believe! Only believe! All things are possible;
only believe." There is something very remarkable about that chorus. God wants to
impress it so deeply on our hearts that in our cor-
ners, rooms, and private places, we will get en-
grossed in this divine truth: if we will only believe,
He can get in us and out of us for others what otherwise would never be possible. Oh, for this truth to
grab hold of us so that God will come to us afresh
and say, "Only believe." Beloved, this song will help
you. I trust the Lord will give me something to make
you ready for everything so that you will be on God's
schedule and in the place He has designed for you.

The possibilities are within the reach of all. Let
us consider the words from Matthew 16:13: *"He
asked His disciples, saying, 'Who do men say that I,
the Son of Man, am?'"* The response is found in
verse sixteen: *"Simon Peter answered and said, 'You
are the Christ, the Son of the living God.'"*

This is a blessed truth. Lord, help me to convey
it. I am deeply convinced that there is such a marvelous work done in our hearts when the presence of

the Incoming One is revealed. He brings new life in God. Our human souls recognize a tremendous, divine treasure within this truth: that we are in a place where God intends that we will not only be able to bind and loose things on earth and in heaven (v. 19), but also by the grace of God to stand in the situations of the day so that the gates of hell will not be able to triumph against us (v. 18). Beloved, what I desire above all is that my life will be an example in every way of this truth. I want His Word to be a light within me, a flame of fire burning in my bones, presenting itself within my being as reality. God's Word is to be believed in everything that it declares.

Let us read the wonderful words of John 1:12–13:

> *But as many as received Him, to them He gave the right to become children of God, to those who believe in His name: who were born, not of blood, nor of the will of the flesh, nor of the will of man, but of God.*

How marvelous to be born of God and to have His nature. This divine nature came to us as we received the Word of God. And Jesus said to His disciples, *"'Who do men say that I, the Son of Man, am?'...Simon Peter answered and said, 'You are the Christ, the Son of the living God'"* (Matt. 16:13, 16). Peter's response is wonderful. Who do you say that He is? Oh, glory to God, who do you say He is? *"The Christ, the Son of the living God."* The truth comes to us, and we are blessed, *"for flesh and blood has not revealed this...but My Father who is in heaven"* (v. 17). To have this revelation that He is the Son of

God is a revelation that He was manifested to destroy the works of the Devil (1 John 3:8). Sometimes it is important that we encourage one another with these divine relationships. The baptism in the Holy Spirit unfolds not only the operations of God, but also the position we have by the Holy Spirit in this world.

THE ROCK AND THE KEY

My message is to believers, and I know the Lord is going to bless His Word to us. It is a perfect revelation to me and to you. I know that God declares it to us by His own Son. The new birth is a perfect place of royalty where we reign over the powers of darkness, bringing everything to perfect submission to the rightful owner, who is the Lord. He rules within and reigns there, and our bodies have become temples of the Holy Spirit (1 Cor. 6:19).

He said to Peter, *"On this rock I will build My church"* (Matt. 16:18). What rock was it? The rock is the living Word. *"On this rock I will build My church."* Who is the rock? The Son of the living God. He is the rock.

But what are the keys? The keys are the divine working by faith in the things of God. *"And I will give you the keys of the kingdom of heaven"* (v. 19). Remember this: it is the key that has life within it. It is life divine. The key holds the power to enter in. That verse opens and unlocks all the dark things and brings life and liberty to the captive. *"On this rock I will build My church, and the gates of Hades shall not prevail against it"* (v. 18).

Now let us see how it works. It works; it always works; it never fails to work. Now let me bring before you the truth because you know you cannot depend upon yourself in this, so I want to help you. You will never be able to get anything by your own initiative. You cannot do it. It is divine life flowing through you that empowers you to act. You are in the right position when you allow the glory of the new life to cause you to act.

An Interpretation of Tongues:
Out of the depths I cried, and the Lord heard my cry and brought me into a large place on sea, on land, in a large place.

OPPORTUNITY FOR ACTION

On a ship one day, some people said to me, "We are going to have a program. Would you be a participant in the entertainment?"

"Oh, yes, I will be in anything that is going to be helpful," I replied, and I believe God was in it.

So they said to me, "What can you do? What place will you take in the entertainment?"

"I can sing," I offered.

So they said to me, "Where would you like to be scheduled in the entertainment? We are going to have a dance."

I said, "Put me down just before the dance."

That evening, I was longing for my turn to come because there had been a clergyman there trying to sing and entertain them, and it seemed so out of place. My turn came, and I sang: "If I Could Only Tell Him As I Know Him." I sang the song, and when I finished, the people said, "You have spoiled the dance." Well, I was there for that purpose, to spoil the dance.

A preacher came to me afterwards and said, "How dare you sing that?" "Why," I said, "how dare I not sing it?" It was my opportunity. He was going to India, and when he got there, he wrote in his periodical and mailed it to England. He said, "I did not seem to have any chance to preach the Gospel, but there was a plumber on board who seemed to have plenty of opportunities to preach to everybody. He said things that continue to stick with me. He told me that the book of Acts was written only because the apostles acted."

You see, I was in the drama of life-acting in the name of Jesus. And so that opened the door and provided me a place that I could speak all the time. The door was open in every way. Glory to God.

The next morning, a young man and his wife came to me and said, "We are in a terrible state. We are looking after a gentleman and lady in the first class; she is a great teacher of Christian Science. She has been taken seriously ill, and the doctor gives her little hope. We have told her about you, and she said she would like to see you." I said, "All right."

That was my opportunity. Opportunity is a wonderful thing. Opportunity is the great thing of the day. And so when I went into the lady's first-class room, I saw that she was very sick. I said, "I am not going to speak to you about anything, not even about your sickness. I am simply going to lay my hands upon you in the name of Jesus, and the moment I do, you will be healed." As soon as I laid my hands upon her, the fever left her, and she was perfectly healed.

However, she was terribly troubled in her mind and heart, and for three days she became worse. I knew it would have been easy to share the Bread of Life with her and to bring her into liberty, but God would not allow it. Just before she got saved, she felt that she would be lost forever. Then God saved her. Hallelujah.

She asked, "What will I do?"

I said, "What do you mean?"

"Oh," she said, "for three years I have been preaching all over England; we live in a great house in India, and we have a great house in London. I have been preaching Christian Science, and now what can I do? You know my salvation is so real. I am a new woman altogether."

Filled with joy, she said, "Will I be able to continue smoking cigarettes?"

"Yes, smoke as many as ever you can; smoke night and day if you can."

Then she asked, "You know we play cards—bridge and other things. Can I play?"

"Yes, play all night through; go on playing."

And she said, "You know we have a little wine, just a little with our friends in the first-class. Should I give it up?"

"No, drink all you want."

Later, she called a maid to her, and said, "I want you to take this telegram and stop that order for a thousand cigarettes." She called her husband and said, "I cannot go into all these things again."

We do not have to go down to bring Him up or up to bring Him down. He is near to you. He is in your heart. It is a living word of faith that we preach. (See Romans 10:6–8.) God wants you all to know that if you only dare to act upon the divine principle that is written there, the gates of hell will not prevail. Praise the Lord.

REIGNING IN LIFE

And so, beloved, it is for all of us. Do not forget this. Every one of you can know this union, this divine relationship, this great power. It will keep you aware that God has come to reveal that everything is subject to you. Through His grace, you have received the *"gift of righteousness"* to *"reign in life through the One, Jesus Christ"* (Rom. 5:17). It is a lovely phrase—reigning in life through Jesus. Love for the Lord is welling up in my heart.

There are two ways to enter into this divine relationship. I am here to say that it does not matter how many times we have failed. There is one keynote in Pentecost: holiness unto the Lord. I find the association with my Lord brings purity and makes my whole being cry out after God, after holiness. Holiness is power. Holiness unto the Lord. Why do I know this? Because I see Jesus my Lord. I see Him; He is so beautiful.

When Jesus went to the tomb of Lazarus, he saw Mary and her friends weeping. Jesus also wept. He wept because of their grief and unbelief. He could not weep because Lazarus was dead. Jesus was and still is *"the resurrection and the life"* (John 11:25). But their sorrow moved Him to groan in His spirit, and He wept. The sequel to that glorious triumph was the great union with His Father. He said to His Father, *"And I know that You always hear Me, but because of the people who are standing by I said this, that they may believe that You sent Me"* (v. 42).

Oh, the blessedness of the truth. That word moves me tremendously. I know that He hears me. Since I know that He hears me, then I know that I have the petition that I desired (1 John 5:15). Glory to God. Not a power in the world can take that knowledge away from you. Every soul is privileged to go into the Holiest of Holies through the blood of the Lamb.

3

A Face-to-Face
Encounter with God

*Then Jacob was left alone; and a Man wrestled
with him until the breaking of day.*
—Genesis 32:24

ooking back on our spiritual journeys, we
will see that we have held on to our own
way too much of the time. When we come to
the end of ourselves, God can begin to take
control. The Scripture asks: *"Can two walk together,
unless they are agreed?"* (Amos 3:3). We cannot enter into the profound truths of God until we relin-
quish control, for *"flesh and blood cannot inherit the
kingdom of God; nor does corruption inherit incor-
ruption"* (1 Cor. 15:50).

Jacob's name means "supplanter." When Jacob
came to the end of his plans, God had a better plan.
How slow we are to see that there is a better way.

The glory is never so wonderful as when we realize our helplessness, throw down our sword, and
surrender our authority to God. Jacob was a diligent

worker, and he would go through any hardship if he could have his own way. In numerous situations, he had his way; all the while, he was ignorant of how gloriously God preserved him from calamity. There is a good; there is a better, but God has a best, a higher standard for us than we have yet attained. It is a better thing if it is God's plan and not ours.

GOD HAS A PLAN

Jacob and his mother had a plan to secure the birthright and the blessing, but God planned the ladder and the angels. Isaac, Jacob's father, agreed that Jacob should go *"to Padan Aram, to the house of Bethuel* [his] *mother's father"* (Gen. 28:2). On his way there, Jacob rested his head on a stone. In his dream, he saw a *"ladder...and its top reached to heaven"* (v. 12). Above the ladder, Jacob saw God and heard Him say: *"The land on which you lie I will give to you and your descendants"* (v. 13). He also heard God tell him: *"I am with you and will keep you wherever you go, and will bring you back to this land; for I will not leave you"* (v. 15). What a good thing for Jacob that in the middle of carrying out his own plan, God found him at the right place. The trickery to obtain the birthright had not been the honorable thing to do, but here at Bethel, he found that God was with him.

Many things may happen in our lives, but when the veil is lifted and we see the glory of God, His tender compassion covers us all the time. How wonderful to be where God is. Jacob experienced twenty-one years of wandering, fighting, and struggling. Listen to his conversation with his wives:

A Face-to-Face Encounter with God

"Your father has deceived me and changed my wages ten times, but God did not allow him to hurt me" (Gen. 31:7). To his father-in-law, Jacob said:

> *Unless the God of my father...had been with me, surely now you would have sent me away empty-handed. God has seen my affliction and the labor of my hands.* (v. 42)

GOD'S WAY IS BEST

Jacob had been out in the bitter frost at night watching the flocks. He was a thrifty man, a hard worker, a planner, a supplanter. We see supplanters in our world today. They may experience a measure of blessing, but God is not first in their lives. We are not judging them, but there is a better way. It is better than our best. It is God's way. Scripture tells us: *"There is a way that seems right to a man, but its end is the way of death"* (Prov. 16:25).

There is a way that God establishes. In our human planning, we may experience blessings of a kind, but we also undergo trials, hardships, and barrenness that God would have kept from us if we had followed His way. I realize through the anointing of the Holy Spirit that there is a freshness, a glow, a security in God where you can know that God is with you all the time. There is a place to reach where all that God has for us can flow through us to a needy world all the time: *"For as the heavens are higher than the earth, so are My ways higher than your ways, and My thoughts than your thoughts"* (Isa. 55:9).

ALONE WITH GOD

Jacob was given time to think: *"Then Jacob was left alone; and a Man wrestled with him until the breaking of day."* Oh, to be left alone with God! In the context of the Scripture, we read that several things had preceded his being alone. His wives and his children had been sent ahead. His sheep, oxen, camels, and donkeys had gone ahead. He was alone.

Often, you will find that you are left alone. Whether you like it or not, you will be left alone like Jacob was left alone. His wives could not make atonement for him; his children could not make atonement for him; his money was useless to help him.

What made Jacob come to that place of loneliness, weakness, and knowledge of himself? He recalled the memory of the grace with which God had met him twenty-one years before, when he saw the ladder and the angels and heard the voice of God: *"Behold, I am with you and will keep you wherever you go, and will bring you back to this land; for I will not leave you until I have done what I have spoken to you"* (Gen. 28:15). He remembered God's mercy and grace.

He was returning to meet his brother Esau, who had become very rich. Esau had been blessed abundantly in the things of this world. He had authority and power to take all that Jacob had and to take vengeance upon him. Jacob knew this. He also knew that there was only one way of deliverance. What was it? Only God could keep Jacob safe. God had met him twenty-one years before when he had left home empty-handed. Now, he was returning with wives, children, and goods, but he was lean in soul and impoverished in spirit. Jacob said to himself, "If I do not get a blessing from God, I can never meet Esau," and he made up his mind he would not go on until he knew that he had favor with God. Jacob was left alone. Unless we get alone with God, we will surely perish. God intervenes when conflict exists. The way of revelation is plain. The Holy Spirit's plan is so clear that we have to say it was God after all.

Jacob was left alone. He knelt alone. The picture is so real to me. Alone! He began to think. He thought about the ladder and the angels. I think as he began to pray, his tongue stuck to the roof of his mouth. Jacob had to get rid of a lot of things. It had all been Jacob! As he got alone with God, he knew it. If you get alone with God, you will find it to be a place of revelation. Jacob was left alone, alone with God. We stay too long with our relations, our camels, and our sheep. Jacob was left alone. Hour after hour passed. He began to feel the presence of God, but he still had not received the desired blessing.

THE WAY TO VICTORY

If ever God is disappointed with you when you wait in His presence, it will be because you are not fervent. If you are not serious and intense, you disappoint God. If God is with you and you know it, be in earnest. Pray and believe: *"Hold fast the confidence and the rejoicing of the hope firm to the end"* (Heb. 3:6). If you do not, you disappoint God.

Jacob was that way. God said, "You are not real enough; you are not hot enough; you are too ordinary; you are no good to Me unless you are filled with zeal—white hot!" The Angel of the Lord said, *"Let Me go, for the day breaks"* (Gen. 32:26). Jacob knew if God went without blessing him, he could not meet Esau. If you are left alone with God and you cannot get to a place of victory, it is a terrible time. You must never let go, whatever you are seeking—fresh revelation, light for your path, some particular need—never let go. Victory is ours if we are earnest enough. All must pass on; nothing less will please God. *"Let Me go, for the day breaks."* He was wrestling with equal strength. Nothing is obtained that way.

You must always master that with which you are wrestling. If darkness covers you, if a fresh revelation is what you need, or if your mind needs to be relieved, always get the victory. God says you are not earnest enough. You say, "The Word does not say that." But it was in God's mind. In wrestling, the strength is in the neck, chest, and thigh; the thigh is the source of strength. So God touched his thigh. With that strength gone, defeat is sure. What did Jacob do? He hung on. God intends for people to be severed by the power of His power, so hold fast; He will never let go. If we let go, we will fall short.

Jacob said, *"I will not let You go unless You bless me!"* (v. 26). And God blessed him: *"Your name shall no longer be called Jacob, but Israel"* (v. 28). The change of Jacob to Israel was wonderful! Israel! Victory all the time! God is building all the time. God is sufficient all the time. Now Jacob has power over Esau, power over the world, power over the cattle. All is in subjection as he comes out of the great night of trial. The sun rises upon him. Oh, that God may take us on.

What happened after that? Read how God blessed and honored him. Esau meets him. There is no fighting now. What a blessed state of grace! They kiss each other: *"When a man's ways please the LORD, He makes even his enemies to be at peace with him"* (Prov. 16:7).

"What about all these cattle, Jacob?"

"Oh, they are a present."

"I have plenty; I don't want your cattle. What a joy it is to see your face again!"

What a wonderful change! Who caused it? God.

HOLDING ON TO GOD

Could Jacob hold God? Can you hold God? Yes, you can. Sincerity can hold Him, dependence can hold Him, weakness can hold Him, for *"when [you are] weak, then [you are] strong"* (2 Cor. 12:10). I'll tell you what cannot hold Him: self-righteousness cannot hold Him; pride cannot hold Him; assumption cannot hold Him; high-mindedness cannot hold Him—thinking you are something when you are nothing, puffed up in your imagination. You can hold Him in your prayer closet, in the prayer meeting, everywhere: *"If anyone hears My voice and opens the door, I will come in to him and dine with him, and he with Me"* (Rev. 3:20).

Can you hold Him? You may sometimes think that He has left you. Oh, no! He does not leave Jacob, Israel. What changed his name? The wrestling? What changed his name? The holding on, the clinging, the brokenness of spirit? If You do not help me, I am no good, no good for the world's need. I am no longer salt. Jacob obtained the blessing because of

37

the favor of God and his yieldedness to God's will. God's Spirit was working in him to bring him to a place of helplessness. God worked to bring him to Bethel, the place of victory. Jacob remembered Bethel, and through all the trying circumstances, he had kept his vow. (See Genesis 28:20–22.)

When we make vows and keep them, God helps us. We must call upon God and give Him an account of the promise. *"And Jacob called the name of the place Peniel: 'For I have seen God face to face, and my life is preserved'"* (Gen. 32:30). How did he know? Do you know when God blesses you? Do you know when you have victory? Over twenty years later, the vision of the ladder and the angels remained with Jacob.

We must have a perfect knowledge of what God has for us. He knew that he had the favor of God, and that no man could hurt him. Let us in all our seeking see that we have the favor of God. Keep His commandments. Walk in the Spirit. Be tenderhearted and lovable. If we do these things, we will be appreciated by others, and our ministry will be a blessing to those who hear. God bless you. God bless you for Jesus' sake.

4

The Living Word

*When He had come down from the mountain,
great multitudes followed Him. And behold, a leper
came and worshiped Him, saying, "Lord, if You are
willing, You can make me clean." Then Jesus put
out His hand and touched him, saying, "I am
willing; be cleansed." Immediately his
leprosy was cleansed.*
—Matthew 8:1–3

When I read these words, my heart is moved, for I realize that Jesus is just as much present with us as He was in Jerusalem when He walked the earth. How it changes our whole nature as we comprehend what Jesus meant when He said: *"You search the Scriptures, for in them you think you have eternal life; and these are they which testify of Me"* (John 5:39). This living Word is not given to us just because of the narratives or the wonderful parables that Jesus taught, but that we, through it, might be changed. Beloved, His presence is so remarkable that if we will but call on Him, believing that He has the giving of eternal life at His command, we will be changed in body, soul, and spirit.

THE SENTENCE OF DEATH

When Jesus was on earth and beheld suffering humanity, He was moved with compassion. He met the most difficult problems; one of the hardest conditions to meet was leprosy. The moment that leprosy was pronounced upon a person, it meant that he was doomed. Just as there was no remedy at that time for a leper, there is no earthly power that can deliver us from sin. Leprosy was the disease that had a death sentence, and sin means death to the spiritual man unless it is cleansed by the blood of Jesus. Here was a leper with the seal of death on him, and there was only one hope. What was it? If he could come to Jesus, he would be healed. But how could a leper come to Jesus? When a leper came near other people, he had to cry out: *"Unclean! Unclean!"* (Lev. 13:45)—so how could a leper ever get near to Jesus?

The difficulty was tremendous, but when faith lays hold, impossibilities must yield. When we touch the Divine and believe God, sin will drop off; disease will go; circumstances will change. I can almost read the thoughts of the people as they passed by the leper: "You poor leper! If you had been where we were, you would have seen the most remarkable things happen, for people were delivered from all kinds of diseases today." The leper might have asked, "Where were you?" They would have answered, "We have been with Jesus!" Oh, the thrill of life when we have been with Jesus.

WATCHING FOR JESUS

Let me give you a little picture. Every night when Jesus left the disciples and made His way up the mountainside, they would watch Him as far as the eye could see, until He disappeared. On the next day, the crowds would gather and watch for His appearing. They were so taken up with watching for Jesus that when they saw Him coming down the mountain, they could not keep quiet. Their hearts were full of the thought of seeing Him, but where was the leper? The leper, too, had come, but the eyes of the people were not on the leper now. They were watching for Jesus. The leper kept close to the crowd, and as Jesus drew nearer, he began his chant, *"Unclean! Unclean!"*

The crowd immediately moved away from him, leaving the path clear for the leper to be the first to get to Jesus. No one could turn him back. No one could stop a man whose heart was set on reaching Jesus. No power on earth can stop a sinner from reaching the side of the Master, if he has faith that will not be denied. Perhaps some have awful diseases in their bodies, or their souls are far away from God. They have been prayed for, and have prayed themselves, but the thing is not removed, and they are in the place where the leper was. He knew that Jesus could heal him, but how could he get near Him?

Jesus makes one great sweeping statement from that day to this as He says, *"I am willing; be cleansed."* Immediately, the man's leprosy was cleansed.

THE PLACE OF HEALING

When you are in the place God wants you to be, you will be healed. Let go of what is hindering you, and you will be established in God. You do not need to wait for a healing service; you can be healed right where you are. You do not need to wait for an altar call; you can be saved now, right where you are.

We have another narrative of a simple act of faith. Here is a man, a centurion, who is very influential. His expression is lovely. He is a man of authority, having soldiers under him, and he has a servant who is sick. He comes right up beside Jesus and says, *"My servant is lying at home paralyzed, dreadfully tormented"* (Matt. 8:6). And Jesus says to him, *"I will come and heal him"* (v. 7).

ROOM FOR JESUS

Listen. There is a marvelous fact in the Scriptures, which may be hard to understand. Jesus said, *"Foxes have holes and birds of the air have nests, but the Son of Man has nowhere to lay His head"* (v. 20). Is this true? Yes, but at the same time, it is not true. He could have had a dozen beds. Then why did He not use them? For the simple reason that the people loved Jesus and wanted Him, yet they dared not have Him in their house. If He would go to their homes, such convicting truths would fall from His lips that they could not stand in His presence. They wanted this holy, lovely Jesus, this beautiful Nazarene, and yet they did not want Him. Thus the Son of Man did not have any place to lay His head, so He spent His nights on the Mount of Olives.

The centurion said, *"Lord, I am not worthy that You should come under my roof. But only speak a word, and my servant will be healed"* (v. 8). The centurion knew that Jesus did not have to be physically present to heal the sick servant. He believed that just a word from Jesus would be sufficient.

Jesus was amazed at this man's faith, and He told the centurion, *"Go your way; and as you have believed, so let it be done for you"* (v. 13). The servant was healed as Jesus spoke.

But some do not want Jesus to come to their homes, and it is not because they have such great faith. They do not want Him to come because of the changes they would have to make in their lives. They know that if Jesus were to live in their hearts, their lives would be totally transformed. How many there are who refuse salvation because they know they cannot continue to live in the same old ways; therefore, they do not invite Christ to their homes. Beloved, let us not be afraid to ask Him to come in to stay. Ask Him to give you grace to come to Him. It is only a step to Jesus. He is not looking at our unworthiness, but at His worthiness. My whole heart cries out to God that I might touch Him afresh.

CHRIST LIVING WITHIN

The greatest gift to mankind is to be able to say, "Christ lives in me!" How wonderful to have the knowledge that He dwells within. How I praise God for His wonderful Word, the Word that *"became flesh and dwelt among us, and we beheld His glory, the glory as of the only begotten of the Father, full of grace and truth"* (John 1:14). John says:

> *That which was from the beginning, which we have heard, which we have seen with our eyes, which we have looked upon, and our hands have handled, concerning the Word of life.*
> (1 John 1:1)

43

That was their natural knowledge of Him. Jesus came into the world in His human nature. Because of that, they could say they had seen and touched eternal life. In holiness and purity, in majesty and power, the Son of God walked the earth. Everyone who touched Him was healed. When He spoke, it was done. Oh, that we might have the divine knowledge of His greatness, whereby we would be constantly changing, going on *"from glory to glory"* (2 Cor. 3:18), until we grow up into His perfect likeness (Eph. 4:15).

5

Our Living Hope

*Blessed be the God and Father of our Lord Jesus
Christ, who according to his abundant mercy has
begotten us again to a living hope through
the resurrection of Jesus Christ from the dead.*
—1 Peter 1:3

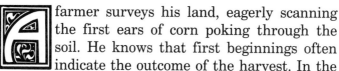farmer surveys his land, eagerly scanning the first ears of corn poking through the soil. He knows that first beginnings often indicate the outcome of the harvest. In the same manner, we can be assured of resurrection because Jesus Christ has risen from the dead. And *"as He is, so are we in this world"* (1 John 4:17). Christ is now getting the church ready for translation. In Peter, we read that we are *"begotten...again to a living hope through the resurrection of Jesus Christ from the dead."* Oh, to be changed. Just as in the flesh Jesus triumphed by the Spirit, we can be like Him in His victory. What a living hope He gives!

Although Paul and Peter were together very little, they both were inspired to bring before the church the vision of this wonderful truth that the living are being changed. If Christ did not rise, our faith is vain. We are still in our sins (1 Cor. 15:17). But Christ has risen and become the firstfruits (v. 23), and we now have the glorious hope that we will also be changed. We who were *"not a people…are now the people of God"* (1 Pet. 2:10). We have been lifted from the mire to be among princes. Beloved, God wants us to see the preciousness of it. It will drive away the dullness of life. Jesus gave all for this treasure. He purchased the field because of the pearl, *"the pearl of great price"* (Matt. 13:46)—the lowest level of humanity. Jesus purchased it, and we are the pearl of great price for all time. Our inheritance is in heaven, and in 1 Thessalonians 4:18, we are told to *"comfort one another with these words."*

What could be better than the hope that in a little while, the change will come? It seems like such a short time ago that I was a boy. Soon, I will be changed by His grace and be more than a conqueror with *"an inheritance incorruptible and undefiled and that does not fade away"* (1 Pet. 1:4). The inheritance is in you. It is something that is accomplished by God for you. When my daughter was in Africa, she often wrote of things corroding. We have a corruptible nature, but as the natural decays, the spiritual is at work. As the corruptible is doing its work, we are changing.

When will it be seen? When Jesus comes. Most beautiful of all, we will be like Him. What is the process? Grace! What can work it out? Love! It cannot be translated into human phrases. God so loved that He gave Jesus (John 3:16).

There is something very wonderful about being undefiled in the presence of my King, never to change, only to be more beautiful. Unless we know something about grace and the omnipotence of His love, we will never be able to grasp it. But believers can say:

> Love, fathomless as the sea.
> Grace flowing for you and for me.

OUR PLACE IS RESERVED

He has prepared a beautiful place for us, and we will have no fear of anyone else taking it; it is reserved. When I went to certain meetings, I would have a reserved seat. I could walk in at any time, and my seat would be unoccupied. What is good about having a reservation? You have a place where you can see Him; it is the very seat you would have chosen. He knows just what you want! He has designed the place for you. Because of His love, you will have joy instead of discord throughout eternity. Will you be there? Is it possible to miss it? We *"are kept by the power of God through faith for salvation ready to be revealed in the last time"* (1 Pet. 1:5).

What is distinctive about it? It will be the fullness of perfection, the ideal of love. The poor in spirit, the mourners, the meek, the hungry and thirsty, the merciful, the pure—all will be ready to be revealed at the appearing of Jesus Christ. You could not remain there unless you had experienced His purifying, perfecting, and establishing. You will be ready when His perfect will has been worked out in you. When you are refined enough, you will go. But there is something to be done yet to establish you, to make you purer. A great price has been paid:

"The genuineness of your faith [is] *much more precious than gold that perishes"* (v. 7). And we must give all and yield all as our Great Refiner puts us in the melting pot again and again. He does this so that we will lose the chaff (Matt. 3:12), so that the pure gold of His presence will be clearly seen, and His glorious image will be reflected. We must be steadfast and immovable, until all His purposes are worked out.

STANDING FIRM THROUGH TRIALS

Praising God in a meeting is a different thing than thanking Him for the trials you face in your life. There must be no perishing though we are tried by fire. What is going to appear at the appearing of Jesus? Faith! Your heart will be established by the grace of the Spirit, which doesn't crush, but refines; doesn't destroy, but enlarges. Oh, beloved, the Enemy is a defeated foe, and Jesus not only conquers but displays the spoils of His conquest. The pure in heart will see God (Matt. 5:8). *"If therefore your eye is good, your whole body will be full of light"* (Matt. 6:22).

What is it? It is loyalty to the Word by the power of the blood. You know your inheritance within you is more powerful than all that is without. How many have gone to the stake and through fiery persecution? Did they desire it? Faith tried by fire had power to stand all ridicule, all slander. We need to have the faith of the Son of God, *"who for the joy that was set before Him endured the cross"* (Heb. 12:2). Oh, the joy of pleasing Him. No trial, no darkness, nothing is too hard for me. If only I may see the image of my Lord again and again. In the melting pot, He removes the skimmings until His face is seen. When the metal reflects Him, it is pure. Who is looking into our hearts? Who is the Refiner? My Lord. He will remove only what will hinder. Oh, I know the love of God is working in my heart.

GETTING READY FOR REVIEW

I remember going to the Crystal Palace when General Booth had a review of representatives of the Salvation Army from all nations. It was a grand sight as company after company with all their distinctive characteristics passed a certain place where he could view them. It was a wonderful scene. We are going to be presented to God. The trials are getting us ready for the procession and the presentation. We are to be a joy to look at, to be to His praise and glory. No one will be there but those who have been tried by fire. Is it worth it? Yes, a thousand times. Oh, the ecstasy of exalted pleasure. God reveals Himself to our hearts.

Peter speaks of *"sincere love"* (1 Pet. 1:22). What does it mean to have *"sincere love"*? It means that even when you are misused or shamed, it never alters; this love is only more refined, making you more like Him. *"Sincere love"* is full of appreciation for those who do not see eye to eye with you. Jesus illustrated it on the cross when He said, *"Father, forgive them"* (Luke 23:34). And Stephen demonstrated it as he was being stoned. He said, *"Lord, do not charge them with this sin"* (Acts 7:60). *"Sincere love"* is the greatest thing God can give to my heart.

We are saved by an incorruptible power—a process always refining, a grace always enlarging, a glory always increasing. We are neither barren nor unfruitful in the knowledge of our Lord Jesus Christ. *"The spirits of just men made perfect"* (Heb. 12:23) are stored in the treasury of the Most High. We are purified as sons and are to be as holy and blameless as He is. Through all eternity, we will gaze at Him with pure, genuine love. God will be glorified as the song is continuously sung: *"Holy, holy, holy, Lord God Almighty"* (Rev. 4:8).

How can we be sad, or hang our heads, or be distressed? If we only knew how rich we are. May God's name be blessed.

6

Our Risen Christ

We praise God that our glorious Jesus is the risen Christ. Those of us who have tasted the power of the indwelling Spirit know something about how the hearts of those two disciples burned as they walked to Emmaus with the risen Lord as their companion. (See Luke 24:13–31.)

Note the words of Acts 4:31: *"And when they had prayed, the place where they were assembled together was shaken."* There are many churches where they never pray the kind of prayer that you read of here. A church that does not know how to pray and to shout will never be shaken. If you live in a place like that, you might as well write over the threshold: *"Ichabod"—"The glory has departed from Israel!"* (1 Sam. 4:21). It is only when men have learned the secret of prayer, power, and praise that God comes forth. Some people say, "Well, I praise God inwardly," but if there is an abundance of praise in your heart, your mouth cannot help speaking it.

WHAT IS INSIDE WILL COME OUT

A man who had a large business in London was a great churchgoer. The church he attended was

51

beautifully decorated, and his pew was delightfully cushioned—just enough to make it easy to sleep through the sermons. He was a prosperous man in business, but he had no peace in his heart. There was a boy at his business who always looked happy. He was always jumping and whistling. One day he said to this boy, "I want to see you in my office."

When the boy came to his office, the man asked him, "How is it that you can always whistle and be happy?" "I cannot help it," answered the boy. "Where did you get this happiness?" asked the gentleman. "I got it at the Pentecostal mission." "Where is that?" The boy told him, and the man began attending. The Lord reached his heart, and in a short while, he was entirely changed. One day, shortly after this, he found that instead of being distracted by his business as he formerly had been, he was actually whistling. His disposition and his whole life had been changed.

The shout cannot come out unless it is within. The inner working of the power of God must come first. It is He who changes the heart and transforms the life. Before there is any real outward evidence, there must be the inflow of divine life. Sometimes I say to people, "You weren't at the meeting the other night." They reply, "Oh, yes, I was there in spirit." I say to them, "Well, next time come with your body also. We don't want a lot of spirits here and no bodies. We want you to come and get filled with God." When all the people come and pray and praise as did these early disciples, there will be something happening. People who come will catch fire, and they will want to come again. But they will have no use for a place where everything has become formal, dry, and dead.

The power of Pentecost came to loose men. God wants us to be free. Men and women are tired of imitations; they want reality; they want to see people who have the living Christ within, who are filled with Holy Spirit power.

GOD IS ALWAYS ON TIME

I received several letters and telegrams about a certain case, but when I arrived I was told I was too late. I said, "That cannot be. God has never sent me anywhere too late." God showed me that something different would happen than anything I had ever seen before. The people I went to were all strangers. I was introduced to a young man who lay helpless, and for whom there was no hope. The doctor had been to see him that morning and had declared that he would not live through the day. He lay with his face to the wall, and when I spoke to him, he whispered, "I cannot turn over." His mother said that they had had to lift him out of bed on sheets for weeks, and that he was so frail and helpless that he had to stay in one position.

The young man said, "My heart is so weak." I assured him, *"God is the strength of* [your] *heart and* [your] *portion forever'* (Ps. 73:26). If you will believe God, it will be so today."

Our Christ is risen. He is a living Christ who lives within us. We must not have this truth merely as a theory. Christ must be risen in us by the power of the Spirit. The power that raised Him from the dead must animate us, and as this glorious resurrection power surges through our beings, we will be freed from all our weaknesses. We will *"be strong in the Lord and in the power of His might"* (Eph. 6:10). There is a resurrection power that God wants you to have and to have today. Why not receive your portion here and now?

I said to these people, "I believe your son will rise today." They only laughed. People do not expect to see signs and wonders today as the disciples saw them of old. Has God changed? Or has our faith diminished so that we are not expecting the greater works that Jesus promised? We must not sing in any minor key. Our message must rise to concert pitch, and there must be nothing left out of it that is in the Book.

It was wintertime, and I said to the parents, "Will you get the boy's suit and bring it here?" They would not listen to the request, for they were expecting the boy to die. But I had gone to that place believing God. We read of Abraham:

> *(As it is written, "I have made you a father of many nations") in the presence of Him whom he believed; God...gives life to the dead and calls those things which do not exist as though they did.* (Rom. 4:17)

God, help us to understand this. It is time people knew how to shout in faith as they contemplate the eternal power of our God, to whom it is nothing to *"give life to your mortal bodies"* (Rom. 8:11) and raise the dead. I come across some who would be giants in the power of God, but they have no shout of faith. Everywhere, I find people who become discouraged even when they are praying simply because they are just breathing sentences without uttering speech. You cannot win the victory that way. You must learn to take the victory and shout in the face of the Devil, "It is done!" There is no man who can doubt if he learns to shout. When we know how to shout properly, things will be different, and tremendous things will happen. In Acts 4:24 we read, *"they raised their voice to God with one accord."* It surely must have been a loud prayer. We must know that God means for us to have life. If there is anything in the world that has life in it, it is this Pentecostal revival we are in. I believe in the baptism of the Holy Spirit with the speaking in tongues, and I believe that every man who is baptized in the Holy Spirit will *"speak with other tongues, as the Spirit* [gives him] *utterance"* (Acts 2:4). I believe in the Holy Spirit. And if you are filled with the Spirit, you will be superabounding in life, and living waters will flow from you.

At last I persuaded the parents to bring the boy's clothes and lay them on the bed. From the human viewpoint, the young man lay dying. I spoke to the afflicted one, "God has revealed to me that as I lay my hands on you, the place will be filled with the Holy Spirit, the bed will be shaken, and you will be shaken and thrown out of bed. By the power of the Holy Spirit, you will dress yourself and be strong." I said this to him in faith. I laid hands on him in the name of Jesus, and instantly the power of God fell and filled the place. I felt helpless and fell flat on the floor. I knew nothing except that a short while after, the place was shaken. I heard the young man walking over to me, saying, "For Your glory, Lord! For Your glory, Lord!"

He dressed himself and cried, "God has healed me." The father fell, the mother fell, and another who was present fell also. God manifested His power that day in saving the whole household and healing the young man. It is the power of the risen Christ we need. Today, that young man is preaching the Gospel.

GOD IS AT WORK

For years we have been longing for God to come forth, and, praise Him, He is coming forth. The tide is rising everywhere. I was in Switzerland not long ago, preaching in many places where the Pentecostal message had not been heard. Today, there are nine new Pentecostal assemblies in different places going on blessedly for God. All over the world it is the same; this great Pentecostal work is in motion. You can hardly go to a place now where God is not pouring out His Spirit upon all flesh, and His promises never fail. Our Christ is risen. His salvation was not a thing done in a corner. Truly He was a man of glory who went to Calvary for us in order that He might free us from all that would mar and hinder, that He might transform us by His grace and bring us out from under the power of Satan into the glorious power of God. One touch of our risen Christ will raise the dead. Hallelujah!

Oh, this wonderful Jesus of ours comes and indwells us. He comes to abide. It is He who baptizes us with the Holy Spirit and makes everything different. We are to be a *"kind of firstfruits"* (James 1:18) unto God and are to be like Christ who is the firstfruit. We are to walk in His footsteps and live in

His power. What a salvation this is, having this risen Christ in us. I feel that everything else must go to nothingness, helplessness, and ruin. Even the best thought of holiness must be on the decrease in order that Christ may increase. All things are under the power of the Spirit.

GOD IS WITH YOU

Dare you take your inheritance from God? Dare you believe God? Dare you stand on the record of His Word? What is the record? If you will believe, you will see the glory of God. You will be sifted as wheat. You will be tested as though some strange thing tried you. You will be put in places where you will have to put your whole trust in God. There is no such thing as anyone being tested beyond what God will allow. There is no temptation that will come, but God will be with you right in the temptation to deliver you (1 Cor. 10:13), and when you have been tried, He will bring you forth as gold (Job 23:10). Every trial is to bring you to a greater position in God. The trial that tries your faith will take you on to the place where you will know that the faith of God will be forthcoming in the next test. No man is able to win any victory except through the power of the risen Christ within him. You will never be able to say, "I did this or that." You will desire to give God the glory for everything.

If you are sure of your ground, if you are counting on the presence of the living Christ within, you can laugh when you see things getting worse. God wants you to be settled and grounded in Christ and to become steadfast and unmoveable in Him. The

Lord Jesus said, *"I have a baptism to be baptized with, and how distressed I am till it is accomplished!"* (Luke 12:50). Assuredly, He was obedient to the will of His Father in Gethsemane, in the judgment hall, and, after that, on the cross, where He, *"through the eternal Spirit offered Himself without spot to God"* (Heb. 9:14). God will take us right on in like manner, and the Holy Spirit will lead every step of the way. God led Him right through to the empty tomb, to the glory of the Ascension, to a place on the throne. The Son of God will never be satisfied until He has us with Himself, sharing His glory and sharing His throne.

7

Pressing Through

f anything stirs me in my life, it is words such as these: *"We never saw anything like this!"* (Mark 2:12). These words were spoken following the healing of a paralyzed man. His four friends removed a portion of the roof in order to *"let down the bed on which the paralytic was lying"* (v. 4). Jesus healed the man, and

> *Immediately he arose, took up the bed, and went out in the presence of them all, so that all were amazed and glorified God, saying, "We never saw anything like this!"* (v. 12)

Something should happen all the time to cause people to say, "We never saw anything like that." God is dissatisfied with stationary conditions. So many people stop at the doorway when God in His great plan is inviting them into His treasury. He opens the storehouse of the Most High, *"the unsearchable riches of Christ"* (Eph. 3:8), to us. God wants to move us into this divine position so that we are completely new creations (2 Cor. 5:17). You

59

know that the flesh profits nothing. Paul says in Romans that *"the carnal mind is enmity against God; for it is not subject to the law of God, nor indeed can be"* (8:7). As we cease to live in the old life and come to know the resurrection power of the Lord, we enter a place of rest, faith, joy, peace, blessing, and life everlasting. Glory to God!

May the Lord give us a new vision of Himself and fresh touches of divine life. May His presence shake off all that remains of the old life and bring us fully into His newness of life. May He reveal to us the greatness of His will concerning us, for there is no one who loves us like Him. Yes, beloved, there is no love like His, no compassion like His. He is filled with compassion and never fails to take those who will fully obey Him into the Promised Land.

THE SWEET PRESENCE OF GOD

In God's Word, there is always more to follow, always more to know. If only we could be like children in taking in the mind of God, what wonderful things would happen. Do you apply the whole Bible to your life? It is grand. Never mind those who take only a part. You take it all. When we get such a thirst that nothing can satisfy us but God, we will have a royal time.

The child of God must have reality all the time. After the child of God comes into the sweetness of the perfume of the presence of God, he will have the hidden treasures of God. He will always be feeding on that blessed truth that will make life full of glory. Are you dry? There is no dry place in God, but all good things come out of hard times. The harder the place you are in, the more blessing can come out of it as you yield to His plan. Oh, if only I had known God's plan in its fullness, I might never have had a tear in my life. God is so abundant, so full of love and mercy; there is no lack to those who trust in Him. I pray that God will give us a touch of reality, so that we may be able to trust Him all the way.

It is an ideal thing to get people to believe that when they ask, they will receive (Matt. 21:22). But how could it be otherwise? It must be so when God says it. Now we have a beautiful word brought before us in the case of this paralyzed man, helpless and so weak that he could not help himself get to Jesus. Four men, whose hearts were full of compassion, carried the man to the house, but the house was full. Oh, I can see that house today as it was filled, jammed, and crammed. There was no room, even by the door. It was crowded inside and out.

THE WAY TO JESUS

The men who were carrying the sick man said, "What will we do?" But there is always a way. I have never found faith to fail, never once. May the Holy Spirit give us a new touch of faith in God's unlimited power. May we have a living faith that will dare to trust Him and say, "Lord, I do believe."

There was no room, *"not even near the door"* (Mark 2:2), but these men said, "Let's go up on the roof." Unbelieving people would say, "Oh, that is silly, ridiculous, foolish!" But men of faith say, "We must get our friend help at all costs. It is nothing to move the roof. Let's go up and go through." Lord, take us today, and let us go through; let us drop right into the arms of Jesus. It is a lovely place to drop into, out of your self-righteousness, out of your self-consciousness, out of your unbelief. Some people have been in a strange place of deadness for years, but God can shake them out of it. Thank God, some of the molds have been broken. It is a blessed thing when the old mold gets broken, for God has a new mold. He can perfect the imperfect by His own loving touch.

PAID IN FULL

I tell you, friends, that since the day that Christ's blood was shed, since the day of His atonement, He has paid the price to meet all the world's needs and its cries of sorrow. Truly Jesus has met the needs of broken hearts and sorrowful spirits, withered limbs and broken bodies. God's dear Son paid the debt for all, for He *"took our infirmities and bore our sicknesses"* (Matt. 8:17). He was *"in all points tempted as we are, yet without sin"* (Heb. 4:15). I rejoice to bring Him to you today, even though it is in my crooked Yorkshire speech, and say to you that He is the only Jesus; He is the only plan; He is the only life; He is the only help; but thank God, He has triumphed to the utmost. He came *"to seek and to save that which was lost"* (Luke 19:10), and He heals all who come to Him.

As the paralyzed man was lowered through the roof, there was a great commotion, and all the people gazed up at this strange sight. We read: *"When Jesus saw their faith, He said to the paralytic, 'Son, your sins are forgiven you'"* (Mark 2:5). What had the forgiveness of sins to do with the healing of this man?

It had everything to do with it. Sin is at the root of disease. May the Lord cleanse us from outward sin and from inbred sin and take away all that hinders the power of God to work through us.

"Some of the scribes were sitting there and reasoning in their hearts" (v. 6). They asked: *"Who can forgive sins but God alone?"* (v. 7). But the Lord answered the thoughts of their hearts by saying,

> *"Which is easier, to say to the paralytic, 'Your sins are forgiven you,' or to say, 'Arise, take up your bed and walk'? But that you may know that the Son of Man has power on earth to forgive sins;" He said to the paralytic, "I say to you, arise, take up your bed, and go to your house."* (vv. 9–11)

Jesus healed that man. He saw also the faith of the four men. There is something in this for us today. Many people will not be saved unless some of you are used to stir them up. Remember that you are your *"brother's keeper"* (Gen. 4:9). We must take our brother to Jesus. When these men carried the paralyzed man, they pressed through until he could hear the voice of the Son of God, and liberty came to the captive. The man became strong by the power of God, arose, took up his bed, and went forth before them all.

I have seen wonderful things like this accomplished by the power of God. We must never think about our God in small ways. He spoke the word one day and made the world. That is the kind of God we have, and He is just the same today. There is no change in Him. Oh, He is lovely and precious above all thought and comparison. There is none like Him.

CLAIM HIS PROMISES

I am certain today that nothing will profit you but what you take by faith. As you *"draw near to God...He will draw near to you"* (James 4:8). Believe and claim the promises, for they are *"Yes"* and *"Amen"* to all who believe (2 Cor. 1:20). Let us thank God for this full Gospel, which is not hidden under a bushel today (Matt. 5:15). Let us thank Him that He is bringing out the Gospel as *"in the days of His flesh"* (Heb. 5:7). All the time, God is working right in the very middle of us, but I want to know, what are you going to do with the Gospel today? There is a greater blessing for you than you have ever received in your life. Do you believe it? Will you receive it?

8

Righteousness

*You have loved righteousness
and hated lawlessness;
therefore God, Your God
has anointed You with the oil of gladness
more than Your companions.*
—Hebrews 1:9

As we are filled with the Holy Spirit, God purposes that like our Lord, we should love righteousness and hate lawlessness. I see that there is a place for us in Christ Jesus where we are no longer under condemnation but where the heavens are always open to us. I see that God has a realm of divine life opening up to us where there are boundless possibilities, where there is limitless power, where there are untold resources, and where we have victory over all the power of the Devil. I believe that, as we are filled with the desire to press on into this life of true holiness, desiring only the glory of God, nothing can hinder our true advancement.

PRECIOUS FAITH

Peter begins his second letter with these words:

*Simon Peter, a bondservant and apostle of Je-
sus Christ, to those who have obtained like
precious faith with us by the righteousness of
our God and Savior Jesus Christ.* (2 Pet. 1:1)

Through faith, we realize that we have a blessed
and glorious union with our risen Lord. When He
was on earth, Jesus told us, *"I am in the Father and
the Father in Me"* (John 14:11). *"The Father who
dwells in Me does the works"* (v. 10). And He prayed
to His Father, not only for His disciples, but for
those who would believe on Him through their testimonies: *"that they all may be one, as You, Father,
are in Me, and I in You; that they also may be one in
Us, that the world may believe that You sent me"*
(John 17:21). What an inheritance is ours when the
very nature, the very righteousness, the very power
of the Father and the Son are made real in us. This
is God's purpose, and as by faith, we take hold of the
purpose, we will always be conscious that *"He who is
in* [us] *is greater than he who is in the world"* (1
John 4:4). The purpose of all Scripture is to move us
to this wonderful and blessed elevation of faith
where our constant experience is the manifestation
of God's life and power through us.

Peter goes on writing to those who have obtained *"like precious faith,"* saying, *"Grace and peace
be multiplied to you in the knowledge of God and of
Jesus our Lord"* (2 Pet. 1:2). We can have the multi-
plication of this grace and peace only as we live in

the realm of faith. Abraham attained to the place where he became a *"friend of God"* because he *"believed God"* (James 2:23). He *"believed God, and it was accounted to him for righteousness"* (v. 23). Righteousness was credited to him on no other ground than that he *"believed God."* Can this be true of anybody else? Yes, it can be true for every person in the whole wide world who is saved and is blessed along with faithful Abraham. The promise that came to him because of his faith was that in him all the families of the earth would be blessed (Gen. 18:18). When we believe God, there is no telling where the blessings of our faith will end.

Some are anxious because, when they are prayed for, the thing that they are expecting does not happen that same night. They say they believe, but you can see that they are really in turmoil from their unbelief. Abraham believed God. You can hear him saying to Sarah, "Sarah, there is no life in you, and there is nothing in me; but God has promised us a son, and I believe God." That kind of faith is a joy to our Father in heaven.

EYES OF FAITH

One day I was having a meeting in Bury, in Lancashire, England. A young woman from a place called Ramsbottom came to be healed of an enlargement of her thyroid gland. Before she came she said, "I am going to be healed of this goiter, Mother." After one meeting she came forward and was prayed for. The next meeting she got up and testified that she had been wonderfully healed. She said, "I will be so happy to go and tell Mother about my healing."

She went to her home and testified how wonderfully she had been healed. The next year when we were having the convention, she came again. From a human perspective, it looked as though the goiter was just as big as ever, but that young woman was believing God. Soon she was on her feet giving her testimony, saying, "I was here last year, and the Lord wonderfully healed me. I want to tell you that this has been the best year of my life." She seemed to be greatly blessed in that meeting, and she went home to testify more strongly than ever that the Lord had healed her.

She believed God. The third year, she was at the meeting again, and some people who looked at her said, "How big that goiter has become." But when the time came for testimonies, she was on her feet and testified, "Two years ago, the Lord gloriously healed me of a goiter. Oh, I had a most wonderful healing. It is grand to be healed by the power of God." That day someone questioned her and said, "People will think there is something the matter with you. Why don't you look in the mirror? You will see your goiter is bigger than ever." The young woman went to the Lord about it and said, "Lord, You so wonderfully healed me two years ago. Won't You show all the people that You healed me?" She went to sleep peacefully that night still believing God. When she came down the next day, there was not a trace or a mark of that goiter.

THE MIRROR OF FAITH

God's Word is from everlasting to everlasting. His Word cannot fail. God's Word is true, and when we rest in its truth, what mighty results we can get. Faith never looks in the mirror. The mirror of faith is the perfect law of liberty:

> *But he who looks into the perfect law of liberty and continues in it, and is not a forgetful hearer but a doer of the work, this one will be blessed in what he does.* (James 1:25)

To the man who looks into this perfect law of God, all darkness is removed. He sees his completeness in Christ. There is no darkness in faith. Darkness is only in nature. Darkness exists when the natural replaces the divine.

Grace and peace are multiplied to us through a knowledge of God and of Jesus Christ. As we really know our God and Savior, we will have peace multiplied to us like the multiplied fires of ten thousand Nebuchadnezzars. (See Daniel 3:10–30.) Our faith will increase even though we are put into a den of lions, and we will live with joy in the middle of the whole thing. What was the difference between Daniel and the king that night when Daniel was put into the den of lions? Daniel's faith was certain, but the king's was experimental. The king came around the next morning and cried, *"Daniel, servant of the living God, has your God, whom you serve continually, been able to deliver you from the lions?"* (Dan. 6:20). Daniel answered, *"My God sent His angel and shut the lions' mouths"* (v. 22). The thing was done. It was done when Daniel prayed with his windows open toward heaven. All our victories are won before we go into the fight. Prayer links us to our lovely God, our abounding God, our multiplying God. Oh, I love Him. He is so wonderful!

HOLINESS OPENS THE DOOR

You will note as you read 2 Peter 1:1–2 that this grace and peace are multiplied through the knowledge of God, but that first our faith comes through the righteousness of God. Note that righteousness comes first and knowledge afterwards. It cannot be otherwise. If you expect any revelation of God apart from holiness, you will have only a mixture. Holiness opens the door to all the treasures of God. He must first bring us to the place where we, like our Lord, "[love] *righteousness and* [hate] *lawlessness,"* before He opens up to us these good treasures. When we *"regard iniquity in* [our hearts], *the Lord will not hear"* us (Ps. 66:18), and it is only as we are made righteous, pure, and holy through the precious blood of God's Son that we can enter into this life of holiness and righteousness in the Son. It is the righteousness of our Lord Himself made real in us as our faith remains in Him.

After I was baptized with the Holy Spirit, the Lord gave me a blessed revelation. I saw Adam and Eve turned out of the Garden for their disobedience. They were unable to partake of the Tree of Life, for the cherubim with flaming sword kept them away from this tree. When I was baptized, I saw that I had begun to eat of this Tree of Life, and I saw that the flaming sword surrounded it. It was there to keep the Devil away. Oh, what privileges are ours when we are born of God. How marvelously He keeps us so that the Wicked One cannot touch us. I see a place in God where Satan cannot come. We are *"hidden with Christ in God"* (Col. 3:3). He invites us all to come and share this wonderful hidden place. We dwell *"in*

the secret place of the Most High" and *"abide under
the shadow of the Almighty"* (Ps. 91:1). God has this
place for you in this blessed realm of grace.

Peter goes on to say:

> *As His divine power has given to us all things
> that pertain to life and godliness, through the
> knowledge of Him who called us by glory and
> virtue, by which have been given to us exceed-
> ing great and precious promises, that through
> these you may be partakers of the divine na-
> ture.* (2 Pet. 1:3–4)

DARE TO BELIEVE GOD

"Faith is the substance of things hoped for"
(Heb. 11:1) right here in this life. It is here that God
wants us to share in His divine nature. It is nothing
less than the life of the Lord Himself imparted and
flowing into our whole beings, so that our very bodies are quickened, so that every tissue, every drop of
blood, and our bones, joints, and marrow receive this
divine life. I believe that the Lord wants this divine
life to flow right into our natural bodies. God wants
to establish our faith so that we will grasp this divine life, this divine nature of the Son of God, so that
our *"spirit, soul, and body be preserved blameless at
the coming of our Lord Jesus Christ"* (1 Thess. 5:23).

When the woman who had suffered for twelve
years from a flow of blood was healed, Jesus per-
ceived that power had gone out of Him (Mark 5:25–
34). The woman's faith reached out, and His power
was imparted. Immediately, the woman's being was
charged with life, and her weakness departed. The

conveying of this power produces everything you need, but it comes only as your faith reaches out to accept it. Faith is the victory. If you can believe, the healing power is yours.

I suffered for many years from hemorrhoids, until my whole body was thoroughly weak; the blood used to gush from me. One day I got desperate and took a bottle of oil to anoint myself. I said to the Lord, "Do what You want to, quickly." I was healed at that very moment. God wants us to have an activity of faith that dares to believe God. There is what seems to be faith, an appearance of faith, but real faith believes God right to the end.

What was the difference between Zacharias and Mary? The angel came to Zacharias and told him his wife Elizabeth would bear a son (Luke 1:13). Zacharias began to question this message, saying, *"I am an old man, and my wife is well advanced in years"* (v. 18). Gabriel, the angel of the Lord, rebuked him for his unbelief and told him, *"You will be mute and not able to speak until the day these things take place, because you did not believe my words"* (v. 20).

Note the contrast when the angel came to Mary. She said, *"Behold the maidservant of the Lord! Let it be to me according to your word"* (v. 38). And Elizabeth greeted Mary with the words, *"Blessed is she who believed, for there will be a fulfillment of those things which were told her from the Lord"* (v. 45).

God wants us to believe His Word in the same way. He wants us to come with a boldness of faith, declaring, "You have promised it, Lord. Now do it." God rejoices when we manifest a faith that holds Him to His Word. Can we get there?

Righteousness

FAITH CLAIMS THE VICTORY

The Lord has called us to this glory and power.
As our faith claims His promises, we will see this
evidenced. I remember one day I was holding a
meeting. My uncle came to that meeting and said,
"Aunt Mary would like to see Smith before she dies."
I went to see her, and she was assuredly dying. I
said, "Lord, can't You do something?" All I did was
stretch out my hands and lay them on her. It seemed
as though there was an immediate touch of the glory
and power of the Lord. Aunt Mary cried, "It is going
all over my body." That day she was made perfectly
whole.

One day I was preaching, and a man brought a
boy who was wrapped up in bandages. It was impossible for him to walk, so it was difficult for them to
get him to the platform. They passed him over about
six seats. The power of the Lord was present to heal,
and it entered right into the child as I placed my
hands on him. The child cried, "Daddy, it is going all
over me." They took off the boy's bandages and
found nothing wrong with him.

The Lord wants us to be walking letters of His
Word. Jesus is the Word and is the power in us. It is
His desire to work in and through us *"for His good
pleasure"* (Phil. 2:13). We must believe that He is in
us. There are boundless possibilities for us if we dare
to act in God and dare to believe that the wonderful
power of our living Christ will be made clear
through us as we lay our hands on the sick in His
name (Mark 16:18).

The *"exceedingly great and precious promises"*
(2 Pet. 1:4) of the Word are given to us that we

might be *"partakers of the divine nature"* (v. 4). I feel the Holy Spirit is grieved with us when we know these things but do not do greater deeds for God. Does not the Holy Spirit show us wide-open doors of opportunity? Will we not let God lead us to greater things? Will we not believe God to take us on to greater demonstrations of His power? He calls us to forget the things that are behind, reach toward the things ahead, and *"press toward the goal for the prize of the upward call of God in Christ Jesus"* (Phil. 3:13–14).

9

Uttermost Salvation

any people say that the fifth chapter of Matthew is for the millennial age and that people cannot live it now. Consequently, they avoid this chapter without carefully investigating it. But for the spiritually mature, there is a little heaven on earth in the truth of this passage. Mature Christians can reach a place where they have no fellowship with darkness and where the world does not know them.

After I was baptized in the Holy Spirit, I saw distinctly that God had allowed me to eat of that Tree of Life of which Adam and Eve were not able to eat. I saw that when the Holy Spirit came in, He wonderfully revealed Christ to me so that I was nourished by His presence, strengthened, and filled with great joy. Praise His name! I know that the baptism of the Holy Spirit brings us into possession of all the fullness of God. People often sing, "Oh, that will be glory for me. When by His grace, I shall look on His face," but I saw that God had changed that song for me so that I can sing:

75

> Oh, now it is glory for me,
> Now it is glory for me,
> For as by His grace,
> I look on His face,
> Now it is glory for me.

A SPIRIT OF POVERTY

Let me come to this wonderful chapter God has given. I will begin with the third verse, *"Blessed are the poor in spirit, for theirs is the kingdom of heaven"* (Matt. 5:3). The people who have grasped this idea and have identified themselves with the Lord Jesus Christ have come to a place where they now see that all things are possible with God. We have come to a place of an unlimited supply in God, and in our poverty of spirit, we are entitled to all that God has, *"for theirs is the kingdom of heaven."* In spite of my meekness, humility, and helplessness, all that God has is mine.

When Jesus came to Sychar, a city of Samaria, *"being wearied from His journey"* (John 4:6), He sat down by a well. His disciples were not with Him because they had gone to buy food in a nearby city (v. 8). When they returned, they saw Him at peace. He was not looking for food but was quite relaxed. When Jesus was not interested in eating the food they had bought, *"the disciples said to one another, 'Has anyone brought Him anything to eat?'"* (v. 33). This shows us the possibility for man to live in God, to be absorbed in God, with no consciousness of the world under any circumstances, except as we bring help to it. And He said to them, *"Behold, I say to you, lift up your eyes and look at the fields, for they are already white for harvest!"* (v. 35). That is His food, the spiritual life in God, which is joy in the Holy Spirit.

He comes to enrapture our souls, to break every bond of mere human affection and replace in us the divine instead of the earthly, the pure instead of the unholy, the eyes of faith that see God instead of human feelings. The divine Son of God is to be in us, mightily moving through us, as we cease to be. This poverty of spirit spoken of in this Beatitude helps us.

A SPIRIT OF MOURNING

We must live in such a pure atmosphere that God will shine in and through our souls. Oh, this uttermost salvation (Heb. 7:25)! I am satisfied that as we get to know the Son of God, we will never be weak anymore. The tide will turn. Let us look at the next verse in Matthew 5: *"Blessed are those who mourn, for they shall be comforted"* (v. 4).

Did Jesus mean mourning over death? No, He meant mourning over our sons and daughters who have not yet reached heaven, who know nothing about the things of the Spirit of Life. When God places within us a mourning cry to move the powers of God, then He will send a revival in every home.

It is impossible to get this spiritual mourning over lost souls without having the very next thing that God says, "[you] *shall be comforted."* As though God could give you a spirit of mourning over a needy soul, then not give you victory! Beloved, it is the mighty power of God in us. And when the Spirit brings us to this mourning attitude over lost souls and over all the failures that we see in professing Christians, until we can go into the presence of God with that mourning spirit, nothing will happen. But when that happens, rejoice; God will bring you through.

A SPIRIT OF MEEKNESS

God wants us to rejoice today. He has brought us into this blessed place that we may mourn and then rejoice. Let us go on with the chapter because much depends on the next verse: *"Blessed are the meek, for they shall inherit the earth"* (Matt. 5:5).

You say, "Don't talk to me about being meek; I will never be able to be like that." Take the case of Moses. He surely was not meek when he killed the Egyptian. But when God got Moses into His hand in the land of Midian, He molded him so that he became the meekest man in all the earth. I do not care what your temper is like. If you get only a little touch of heaven, God can mold you so that you can be the meekest person on the earth.

I used to have such a bad temper that it made me tremble all over. It would make me furious with its evil power. I saw that this temper had to be destroyed; it could not be patched up. One day the power of God fell upon me. I came to the meeting and fell down before the Lord. The people began asking, "What sin has Wigglesworth been committing?" This went on for two weeks. Every time I came to the altar, God used to sweep through me with such a manifestation of my helplessness that I would go down before God and weep right through. Then the preacher or the leader was broken up and came beside me. God started a revival that way. God had broken me up, and revival began through His revival in me. Oh, it was lovely! At last my wife said, "Since my husband had that touch, I have never been able to cook anything that he was not pleased with. It is never too cold and never too hot."

Only God can make people right. Only melted gold is minted. Only moistened clay accepts the mold. Only softened wax receives the seal. Only broken, contrite hearts receive the mark as the Potter turns us on His wheel. Oh, Lord, give us that blessed state where we are perfectly and wholly made meek.

A SPIRIT OF HUNGER AND THIRST

What a wonderful chapter this is. The Beatitudes of the Spirit are truly lovely. *"Blessed are those who hunger and thirst for righteousness, for they shall be filled"* (Matt. 5:6). Oh, yes, praise the Lord! We must emphasize that God will not fail to fill us. No man can *"hunger and thirst after righteousness"* unless God has put the desire in him. And I want you to notice that this righteousness is the righteousness of Jesus.

In 1 John 5:4–5, we find these verses: *"This is the victory that has overcome the world; our faith. Who is he who overcomes the world, but he who believes that Jesus is the Son of God?"* Righteousness is more than paying our way. We hear someone say, "Oh, I never do anything wrong to anybody. I always pay my way." This is simply life in the flesh, but there is a higher *"law of the Spirit of life in Christ Jesus"* (Rom. 8:2). I must see that Jesus is my perfect righteousness. He came by the power of God:

> *For what the law could not do in that it was weak through the flesh, God did by sending*

His own Son in the likeness of sinful flesh, on
account of sin: He condemned sin in the flesh.
(Rom. 8:3)

We must see that if we get this righteousness of
God, sin is destroyed. There are beautiful words in
the ninth verse of the first chapter of Hebrews: *"You*
have loved righteousness and hated lawlessness;
therefore God, Your God, has anointed You with the
oil of gladness more than Your companions."

But the climax of divine touches of heaven never
leaves you stationary but rather increases your
thirst and appetite for greater things. Something
within makes you press on until you are empty of
everything else so that you may be filled with what
God is pressing in. This righteousness is a walk with
God. It is a divine inheritance. It is seeing the face of
Jesus until you cannot be satisfied without drinking
of His Spirit and being overflowed continually with
His blessings. I cannot be satisfied without Christ's
righteousness. He gives us thirst for the immensity
of God's power. It is a divine problem that is solved
in only one way: having Him. And having Him, we
have all things.

A Spirit of Mercy

I pray that God will bring you to a death of self
and a life of righteousness, which will please God in
the Spirit. Thus we understand in some measure
what God has for us in the next verse of Matthew 5:
"Blessed are the merciful, for they shall obtain
mercy" (v. 7).

I believe this is truly a spiritual condition, which is higher than the natural law. Sometimes when we talk about mercy, we think of being kind, amiable, or philanthropic toward others. We think those are respected positions. So they are, but the world has that. Beloved, we should have all that, but we should have much more. We will never understand the meaning of the mercy of Jesus until He fills us with Himself. My blessed Lord! Can there ever be one like Him? Can you think of such rarity, such beauty, such self-sacrifice? *"Blessed are the merciful."* We must have heaven's riches to give to souls in poverty. You cannot be filled with the Lord and not be merciful. You cannot have the baptism with power without this supernatural mercy, this divine touch of heaven that stops satanic forces, frees the oppressed, and strengthens the helpless. That is the spirit that God wants to give us. Oh, for heaven to bend down upon us with this deep inward cry for a touch of Him, His majesty, His glory, His might, His power!

It is a very remarkable thing that the merciful always obtain mercy. Look at the measure of this spiritual life: first full, then pressed down, then shaken together, and then running over (Luke 6:38). This divine touch of heaven is lovely. It is the most charming thing on earth, sweeter than all. I am just running over with new wine this morning. God wants you to have this new wine. It thrills the human heart. How it mightily sweeps you right into heaven!

I ask you all, needy souls, whatever you want, to *"come boldly to the throne of grace"* (Heb. 4:16). Come, and the Lord bless you.

10

Count It All Joy

Count it all joy
when you fall into various trials.
—James 1:2

his letter was addressed *"to the twelve tribes which are scattered abroad"* (v. 1). Only one like the Master could stand and say to the people, *"Count it all joy"* when they were disbursed everywhere, driven to their wits' end, and persecuted. The Scriptures say that *"they wandered in deserts and mountains, in dens and caves of the earth"* (Heb. 11:38). These people were separated from each other, but God was with them.

GOD IS FOR YOU

It does not matter where you are if God is with you. He who is for you is a million times greater than all who can be against you (Rom. 8:31). Oh, if by the grace of God, we could only see that the blessings of God's divine power come to us with such sweetness, whispering to us, "Be still, My child. All is well." Be still and see the salvation of the Lord.

What would happen if we learned the secret to asking once and then believing? What an advantage it would be if we could come to a place where we know that everything is within reach of us. God wants us to see that every obstacle can be removed. God brings us into a place where the difficulties are, where the pressure is, where the hard corner is, where everything is so difficult that you know there are no possibilities on the human side. God must do it. All these places are in God's plan. God allows trials, difficulties, temptations, and perplexities to come right along our path, but there is not a temptation or trial that can come to us without God providing a way out (1 Cor. 10:13). You do not have the way out; it is God who can bring you through.

Many saints come to me and want me to pray for their nervous systems. I guarantee there is not a person in the whole world who could be nervous if he or she understood 1 John 4. Let us read verses sixteen through eighteen:

> *And we have known and believed the love that God has for us. God is love, and he who abides in love abides in God, and God in him. Love has been perfected among us in this: that we may have boldness in the day of judgment; because as He is, so are we in this world. There is no fear in love; but perfect love casts out fear, because fear involves torment. But he who fears has not been made perfect in love.*

Let me tell you what perfect love is. The one *"who believes that Jesus is the Son of God"* is the one *"who overcomes the world"* (1 John 5:5). What is the evidence and assurance of salvation? He who believes in his heart on the Lord Jesus (Acts 16:31). Every expression of love is in the heart. When you begin to pour out your heart to God in love, your very being, your whole self, desires Him. Perfect love means that Jesus has taken hold of your intentions, desires, and thoughts and purified everything. Perfect love cannot fear (1 John 4:18).

GOD WILL DELIVER YOU

What God wants is to saturate us with His Word. His Word is a living truth. I would pity one who has gone a whole week without temptation because God tries only the people who are worthy. If you are passing through difficulties, trials are rising, darkness is appearing, and everything becomes so dense you cannot see through, hallelujah! God will see you through. He is a God of deliverance, a God of power. He is near to you if you will only believe. He can anoint you with fresh oil and make your cup run over (Ps. 23:5). Jesus is the *"balm in Gilead"* (Jer. 8:22), the *"rose of Sharon"* (Song 2:1).

I believe that God wants to align us with such perfection of blessing and beauty that we will say, *"Though He slay me, yet will I trust Him"* (Job 13:15). When the hand of God is on you, and the clay is fresh in the Potter's hands, the vessel will be made perfect as you are pliable in God's hands. Only melted gold is minted. Only moistened clay is molded. Only softened wax receives the seal. Only broken, contrite hearts receive the mark as the Potter turns us on His wheel. He can put His stamp on you today. He can mold you anew and change your vision. He can remove the difficulty. The Lord of Hosts is here, waiting for your affection. Remember

His question, *"Simon, son of Jonah, do you love Me more than these?"* (John 21:15). He never lets the chastening rod fall upon anything except what is marring the vessel. If there is anything in you that is not yielded and bent to the plan of the Almighty, you cannot preserve what is spiritual only in part. When the Spirit of the Lord gets perfect control, then we begin to be changed by the expression of God's light in our human frame. The whole body begins to have the fullness of His life manifested until God so has us that we believe all things.

DRAW NEAR TO GOD

If God brings you into oneness and fellowship with the Most High God, your nature will tremble in His presence. But God can chase away all the defects, the unrest, the unfaithfulness, the wavering, and He can establish you with such comfort that you rest in the Holy Spirit by the power of God. God invites us to higher heights and deeper depths; therefore, we can sing:

> Make me better, make me purer,
>   By the fire that refines,
> Where the breath of God is sweeter,
>   Where the brightest glory shines.
> Take me higher up the mountain
>   Into fellowship with Thee,
> In Thy light I'll see the fountain,
>   And the blood that cleanses me.

I am realizing these days that there is a sanctification of the Spirit where the thoughts are holy, where life is beautiful and pure. As you come closer to God, the Spirit reveals His holiness and shows us a new plan for the present and the future. The height and depth, the breadth and length of God's inheritance for us are truly wonderful.

We read in Romans 8:10, *"And if Christ is in you, the body is dead because of sin, but the Spirit is life because of righteousness."* What a vision, beloved. *"The body is dead"* because sin is being judged and destroyed. The whole body is absolutely put to death; consequently, there is His righteousness, His beauty, the life of the Spirit, freedom, and joy. The Spirit lifts the soul into the presence of heaven. Oh, this is glorious.

EXPERIENCE HIS JOY

"Count it all joy when you fall into various trials." Perhaps you have been counting it all sadness until now. Never mind. Tell it to Jesus now. Express your deepest feelings to Him:

> He knows it all, He knows it all,
>   My Father knows, He knows it all,
> The bitter tears, how fast they fall,
>   He knows, my Father knows it all.

Sometimes I change the words to this song. I would like to sing it as I change it:

> The joy He gives that overflows,
>   He knows, my Father knows it all.

Sorrow may come at night, but *"joy comes in the morning"* (Ps. 30:5). So many believers never look up. When Jesus raised Lazarus from the dead, He lifted His eyes and said, *"Father, I thank You that You have heard Me"* (John 11:41). Beloved, God wants us to have some resurrection touch about us. We may enter into things that will bring us sorrow and trouble, but through them, God will bring us to a deeper knowledge of Himself. Never use your human plan when God speaks His Word. You have your cue from an Almighty Source who has all the resources that never fade away. His treasury is past measuring, abounding with extravagances of abundance, waiting to be poured out upon us.

Hear what the Scripture says: *"God...gives to all liberally and without reproach"* (James 1:5). The almighty hand of God comes to our weakness and says, "If you will dare to trust Me and not doubt, I will abundantly satisfy you from the treasure house of the Most High." He forgives, He supplies, He opens the door into His fullness and makes us know that He has done it all. When you come to Him again, He gives you another overflow without measure, an expression of a Father's love.

Who desires anything from God? He can satisfy every need. He satisfies the hungry with good things (Luke 1:53). I believe a real weeping would be good for us. You are in a poor way if you cannot weep. I do thank God for my tears, which help me. I like to weep in the presence of God. I ask you in the name of Jesus, will you cast *"all your care upon Him, for He cares for you"* (1 Pet. 5:7)? I am in great need today; I want an overflow. Come on, beloved, let us weep together. God will help us. Glory to God. How He meets the needs of the hungry!

11

A Living Faith

We appreciate cathedrals and churches, but God does not dwell in temples made by hands but in the sanctuary of the heart. Here is true worship: *"God is Spirit, and those who worship Him must worship in spirit and truth"* (John 4:24). The Father seeks *"such to worship Him"* (v. 23). The church is the body of Christ. Its worship is a heart worship, a longing to come into the presence of God. God sees our hearts and will open our understanding. The Lord delights in His people. He wants us to come to a place of undisturbed rest and peace that is found only in God. Only simplicity will bring us there. As Jesus placed a little child in the middle of the disciples, He said: *"Unless you are converted and become as little children, you will be no means enter the kingdom of heaven"* (Matt. 18:3). He did not mean that we should seek to have a child's mind, but a child's meek and gentle spirit. It is the only place to meet God. He will give us that place of worship.

How my heart cries out for a living faith and a deep vision of God. The world cannot produce it. It is a place where we see the Lord, a place where we pray and know that God hears. We can ask God and believe Him for the answer, having no fear but a living faith to come into the presence of God. *"In* [His] *presence is fullness of joy; at* [His] *right hand are pleasures forevermore"* (Ps. 16:11).

CHANGED BY GOD

God is looking for people He can reveal Himself in. I used to have a tremendous temper, going white with passion. My whole nature was outside God that way. God knew His child could never be of service to the world unless he was wholly sanctified. I was difficult to please at the table. My wife was a good cook, but I could always find something wrong with the meal. I heard her testify in a meeting that after God sanctified me, I was pleased with everything.

I had men working for me, and I wanted to be a good testimony to them. One day, they waited after work was over and said, "We would like that spirit you have." Our human spirit has to be controlled by the Holy Spirit. There is a place of death and life where Christ reigns in the body. Then all is well. This Word is full of stimulation. It is by faith that we come into a place of grace. Then all can see that we have been made new. The Holy Spirit arouses our attention. He has something special to say: if you will believe, you can be sons of God, like Him in character, spirit, longings, and actions until all know that you are His child.

The Spirit of God can change our nature. God is the Creator. His Word is creative, and if you believe, His creative power can change your whole nature.

You can become *"children of God"* (John 1:12). You cannot reach this altitude of faith alone. No man can keep himself. The all-powerful God spreads His covering over you, saying, *"If you can believe, all things are possible to him who believes"* (Mark 9:23). The old nature is so difficult to manage. You have been ashamed of it many times, but the Lord Himself offers the answer. He says, "Come, and I will give you peace and strength. I will change you. I will operate on you by My power, making you a *'new creation'* (2 Cor. 5:17) if you will believe." He invites us to:

> Leave it there, leave it there.
>   Take your burden to the Lord
> And leave it there.

Jesus says, *"Learn from Me, for I am gentle and lowly in heart, and you will find rest for your souls"* (Matt. 11:29). The world has no rest. It is full of troubles, but in Christ, you can move and act in the power of God with a peace that *"surpasses all understanding"* (Phil. 4:7). An inward flow of divine power will change your nature. *"Therefore the world does not know us, because it did not know Him"* (1 John 3:1).

What does it mean? I have lived in one house for fifty years. I have preached from my own doorstep; all around know me. They know me when they need someone to pray, when there is trouble, when they need a word of wisdom. But at Christmas time when they call their friends to celebrate, would they invite me? No. Why? They would say, "He is sure to want a prayer meeting, but we want a dance."

Wherever Jesus came, sin was revealed, and men don't like sin to be revealed. Sin separates us from God forever. You are in a good place when you weep before God, repenting over the least thing. If you have spoken unkindly, you realized it was not like the Lord. Your keen conscience has taken you to prayer. It is a wonderful thing to have a sensitive conscience. When everything is wrong, you cry to the Lord. It is when we are close to God that our hearts are revealed. God intends us to live in purity, seeing Him all the time. How can we?

> *Beloved, now we are children of God; and it has not yet been revealed what we shall be, but we know that when He is revealed, we shall be like Him, for we shall see Him as He is. And everyone who has this hope in Him purifies himself, just as He is pure.* (1 John 3:2–3)

CHRIST'S PRECIOUS SACRIFICE

As the bridegroom is to the bride, our Lord, the Lamb of God, is the hope of the church. He became poor for us that we might be made rich. What an offering! He suffered, He died, He was buried, He rose, and He is coming for us. How we love Him.

I am praying that God will create children in this meeting. *"But as many as received Him, to them He gave the right to become children of God, to those who believe in His name"* (John 1:12). When we believe, we receive Him. When we receive Him, anything can happen: *"With God all things are possible"* (Matt. 19:26).

When I am leaving anywhere by train or ship, people come to see me off; I preach to them. It is

God's plan for me; it is an order. The captain and the stewards hear me. "Oh!" they say. "Another preacher on board." The world thinks there is something wrong with you if you are full of zeal for God. The world does not know us, but we are sons of God and possess His power. As we look to Jesus, our lives are changed. He is God's Son.

No man who sins has power. Sin makes a man weak, taking away his dignity and power. The Holy Spirit gives joy. It is God's plan. Heaven opens. As you pray, you know He hears. As you read the Word of God, it is alive. Remember that sin dethrones, but purity strengthens. Temptation is not sin, but the Devil is a liar and tries to take away peace. You must live in the Word of God. There is *"now no condemnation"* (Rom. 8:1). Who is he that can condemn you? Christ, but He won't condemn you because He died to love you. Don't condemn yourself. If there is anything wrong, come to Christ's blood: *"If we walk in the light as He is in the light, we have fellowship with one another, and the blood of Jesus Christ His Son cleanses us from all sin"* (1 John 1:7).

WITNESSES OF CHRIST

Jesus came to destroy the works of the Devil. You can enter into a new experience with God. All should fear God. He creates in our hearts such a love for Jesus that we are living in a new realm. We are children of God with power, filled with all the fullness of God:

> *Beloved, if our heart does not condemn us, we have confidence toward God. And whatever we*

> *ask we receive from Him, because we keep His*
> *commandments and do those things that are*
> *pleasing in His sight....By this we know that*
> *He abides in us, by the Spirit whom He has*
> *given us.* (1 John 3:21–22, 24)

Paul went on to impart some spiritual gifts. Did Paul give the gifts? No. The Holy Spirit gives gifts, and Jesus gives gifts. No man can give spiritual gifts.

I am here ministering faith. Before leaving home, I received a wire asking if I would go to Liverpool. If I know God is sending me, my faith rises. A woman with cancer and gallstones was very discouraged. The woman said, "I have no hope." "Well," I said, "I have not come from Bradford to go home with a bad report." God said to me, "Establish her in the fact of the new birth." When she had the assurance that her sin was gone and she was born again, she said, "That is everything to me. Cancer is nothing now. I have got Jesus." The battle was won. God delivered her, and she got up and dressed. She was free, happy in Jesus.

When God speaks, you can rely completely on His Word. Will you believe that God makes you His children? Life and immortality are ours in the Gospel. This is our inheritance through the blood of Jesus: life forevermore. Believe, and the Lord will fill you with life so that you will witness for Him as you wait for His return.

12

Keeping the Vision

Nothing really matters if the Lord loves me, and He does, He does. I was describing to a few people last night how God has blessed this ministry with success. His hand has been upon us. I encountered the same kind of thing in Switzerland where there were nine churches formed and another four being formed. I went back there and found all the people praising the Lord. Just as our brother tonight asked the people who were healed through my ministry to stand up, they stood up. The same thing happened—just the same—and people are being healed during my absence. There is the sequel. There is the power manifested.

I told you when I was here before that if this work ceased, you could count on it that the mission had been Wigglesworth's; if it was of God, it would not cease. Humanity is the failure everywhere, but when humanity is filled with God's divinity, there is no such thing as failure, and we know that the baptism of the Holy Spirit is not a failure. There are two sides to the baptism of the Holy Spirit. The first condition is that you possess the baptism; the second condition is that the baptism possesses you. The first has to happen before the second can occur. God can so manifest His divine power that all souls can possess, if they are eligible, this blessed infilling of the baptism of the Holy Spirit. There is no limit to it. It cannot be measured. It is without limit because God is behind it, in the middle of it, and through it.

After reading all of the epistles, I would say that God is through all, under all, and over all in this work. I pray that the Holy Spirit will be with us. I trust that we will witness the demonstration of the Spirit's power, of the anointing that is received, because every person in this place must see the need of being filled with the Holy Spirit. It is important; no, it is more than important. You neglect it at your peril. From time to time, I see people very negligent, cold, and indifferent. After they get filled with the Holy Spirit, they become ablaze for God. I believe God wants the same portion for every soul in this meeting, but even greater than that because we are in the kingdom.

Ministers of God are to be flames of fire, nothing less than flames, nothing less than holy, mighty instruments with burning messages, with hearts full of love, with depths of consecration where God has taken full charge of their bodies, and they exist only to manifest the glory of God. Surely this is the ideal and purpose of this great plan of salvation for man: that we might be *filled with all the fullness of God* (Eph. 3:19). We are called to be ministers of life and instruments pointing to the saving power for humanity. God works mightily in us, proving and manifesting His grace. This glorious baptism is to be a witness of Jesus, and oh, beloved, we must reach the ideal identification with the Master. It is the same baptism, the same power, the same revelation of the King of Kings. God must fill us with this divine, glorious purpose for God. Clearly, we are to be children of God who testify to His power, which fills the earth.

An Interpretation of Tongues:

The Lord is the Life, the Truth, and the manifestation of bringing into life and power of sonship, built upon the Rock, the Rock Christ Jesus, established with the truth of salvation, our heritage, for we have to go forth with ministry of life unto life, and death unto death, for the Holy Spirit is that ministry.

EQUIPPED FOR SERVICE

Beloved, I want us to turn to this wonderful Word of God. I want you to see how we can be equipped with His power. I want you to keep your minds fixed on this fact, for it will help to establish you. It will strengthen you if you think about Paul, who was *"one born out of due time"* (1 Cor. 15:8). Paul was *"a brand plucked from the fire"* (Zech. 3:2), chosen by God to be an apostle to the Gentiles (Eph. 3:1). I want you to see him, first as a persecutor, furious to destroy those who were bringing glad tidings to the people. See how madly he rushed them into prison, urging them to blaspheme that holy name. Then see this man changed by the power of Christ and the Gospel of God. See him divinely transformed by God, filled with the Holy Spirit. As you read the ninth chapter of Acts, you see how special his calling was. In order for Paul to understand how he might be able to minister to the needy, God's Son said to Ananias, *"For I will show him how many things he must suffer for My name's sake"* (Acts 9:16).

You will find that the cup of suffering from heaven is united with a baptism of fire. I don't want you to think I mean suffering with diseases. I mean suffering in persecution, with slander, strife, bitterness, abusive scoldings, and with many other evil ways of suffering; but none of these things will hurt you. Instead, they will kindle a fire of holy ambition. As the Scripture says, *"Blessed are those who are persecuted for righteousness' sake, for theirs is the kingdom of heaven"* (Matt. 5:10).

To be persecuted for Christ's sake is to be united with a blessed people, with those chosen to cry under the altar, *"How long?"* (Rev. 6:9–10). Oh, to know that we may cooperate with Jesus. If we suffer persecution, rejoice in that day. Beloved, God wants witnesses, witnesses of truth, witnesses to the full truth, witnesses to the fullness of redemption, witnesses to the deliverance from the power of sin and disease, witnesses who can claim their territory, because of the eternal power working in them, eternal life beautifully, gloriously filling the body, until the body is filled with the life of the Spirit. God wants us to believe that we may be ministers of that kind.

Read Acts 20. See how Paul was lost in the zeal of his ministry, and see how those first disciples gathered together on the first day of the week to break bread. See their need for breaking bread. As they were gathered together, they were caught up with the ministry. In Switzerland, the people said to me, "How long can you preach to us?" I said, "When the Holy Spirit is upon me, I can preach forever!"

If it were only man's ability or college training, we might be crazy before we began, but if it is the Holy Spirit's ministry, we will be as sound as a bell that has no flaw in it. It will be the Holy Spirit at the first, in the middle, and at the end. I do not want to think of anything during the preaching so that the preaching will reflect nothing except, "Thus says the Lord." The preaching of Jesus is that blessed incarnation, that glorious freedom from bondage, that blessed power that liberates from sin and the powers of darkness, that glorious salvation that saves you from death to life, and from the power of Satan to God.

I see that Paul was lost in this glorious theme. In the middle of Paul's sermon, Eutychus, a young man, was too drowsy to be aware of his surroundings, and he sank into a deep sleep until he fell from the third-story window in which he had been sitting (Acts 20:9). I have often offered a pound note to anyone who fell asleep in my meetings—you can try it if you want to.

TAKE EACH OPPORTUNITY

I want you to notice that he preached from evening to midnight, and in the middle of the night, this thing happened. If you turn to Philippians, you will see a wonderful truth there where Paul says, *"I may attain to the resurrection"* (3:11). Hear the words spoken to Martha, that wonderful saying when Jesus said to her, *"I am the resurrection and the life. He who believes in Me, though he may die, he shall live"* (John 11:25). Paul desired to attain it, and it is remarkable evidence to me that you never attain anything until opportunity comes. On the activity of faith, you will find that God will bring so many things before your notice that you will have no time to think over them. You will jump into them and bring authority by the power of the Spirit. If you took time to think, you would miss the opportunity.

I was in San Francisco riding down the main street one day. I came across a group in the street, so the driver stopped, and I jumped out of the car. Rushing across to where the commotion was, I found, as I broke through the crowd, a body laid on the ground apparently in a tremendous seizure of death. I got down and asked, "What is wrong?" He replied in a whisper, "Cramp." I put my hand underneath his back and said, "Come out in the name of Jesus," and the boy jumped up and ran away. He never even said, "Thank you."

Likewise, you will find out that with the baptism of the Holy Spirit, you will be in a position where you must act because you have no time to think. The Holy Spirit works on the power of divine origin. It is the supernatural, God filling until it becomes a freeing power by the authority of the Almighty. It sees things come to pass that could not come to pass in any other way.

Returning to Paul's position: it is midnight, and death comes as a result of a fall from a window. The first thing Paul does is the most absurd thing to do, yet it is the most practical thing to do in the Holy Spirit: he fell on the young man. Yes, fell on him, embraced him, and left him alive. Some would say he fell on him, crushed life into him, and brought him back. It is the activity of the Almighty. We must see that in any meeting, the Holy Spirit can demonstrate His divine power until we realize that we are in the presence of God.

I want you to understand that the Holy Spirit is in this meeting. This is a meeting where all can be saved, where all can be healed, where the power of the resurrection of Jesus Christ is clearly in evidence, where we see nothing but Jesus. We are here for the importance of impressing on you that this same Jesus is present here.

THE BLESSING OF THE LORD'S SUPPER

I wish every meeting included a celebration of the Lord's Supper. I would love to see the saints gather together at every meeting in order to remember Christ's death, His resurrection, and His ascension. What a thought that Jesus Himself instituted this glorious memorial for us. Oh, that God would let us see that it is *"as often"* (1 Cor. 11:25) as we do it. It is not weekly, not monthly, not quarterly, but *"as often"* as we do it, and in remembrance of Him. What a blessed remembrance it is to know that He took away our sins. What a blessed remembrance to know that He took away my sins and my diseases. What a blessed remembrance to know that *"He always lives to make intercession"* (Heb. 7:25) for the saints—not the sinners. He has left us to do that: *"I pray for them. I do not pray for the world but for those whom You have given Me, for they are Yours"* (John 17:9). He has left us to pray for the world. He is there interceding for us to keep us right, holy, ready, mighty, and filled with Himself so that we might bring the fragrance of heaven to the world's needs. Can we do it? Yes, we can. We can do it.

THE NEED FOR HUMILITY

Let me read this Scripture to you so that we might get our minds perfectly fortified with this blessed truth that God has for us: *"Serving the Lord with all humility"* (Acts 20:19). None of us will be able to be ministers of this new covenant of promise in the power of the Holy Spirit without humility. It seems to me that the way to get up is to get down. It is clear to me that in the measure the death of the Lord is in me, the life of the Lord will abound in me. To me, the baptism of the Holy Spirit is not a goal; it is an infilling that allows us to reach the highest level, the holiest position that it is possible for human nature to reach. The baptism of the Holy Spirit comes to reveal Him who is filled fully with God. So I see that to be baptized with the Holy Spirit is to be baptized into death, into life, into power, into fellowship with the Trinity, where we cease to be and God takes us forever. Paul said, *"I have been crucified with Christ; it is no longer I who live, but Christ lives in me"* (Gal. 2:20). I believe that God wants to put His hand upon us so that we may reach ideal definitions of humility, of human helplessness, of human insufficiency, until we will rest no more upon human plans, but have God's thoughts, God's voice, and God the Holy Spirit to speak to us. Now here is a word for us: *"And see, now I go bound in the spirit"* (Acts 20:22). There is the Word. Is that a possibility? Is there a possibility for a person to align himself so completely with the divine will of God?

Jesus was a man, flesh and blood like us, while at the same time, He was the incarnation of divine authority, power, and majesty of the glory of heaven. He bore in His body the weaknesses of human flesh. He was tempted *"in all points...as we are, yet without sin"* (Heb. 4:15). He is so lovely, such a perfect Savior. Oh, that I could shout "Jesus" in such a way that the world would hear. There is salvation, life, power, and deliverance through His name. But, beloved, I see that *"the Spirit drove Him"* (Mark 1:12), that He was *"led by the Spirit"* (Luke 4:1), and here comes Paul *"bound in the spirit"* (Acts 20:22).

What an ideal condescension of heaven that God should lay hold of humanity and possess it with His holiness, His righteousness, His truth, and His faith so that he could say, *"'I go bound'* (v. 22); I have no choice. The only choice is for God. The only desire or ambition is God's. I am bound with God." Is it possible, beloved?

If you look at the first chapter of Galatians, you will see how wonderfully Paul rose to this state of bliss. If you look at the third chapter of Ephesians, you see how he became *"less than the least of all saints"* (v. 8). In Acts 26, you will hear him say: *"King Agrippa, I was not disobedient to the heavenly vision"* (v. 19). In order to keep the vision, he yielded not to flesh and blood. God laid hold of him; God bound him; God preserved him. I ought to say, however, that it is a wonderful position to be preserved by the Almighty. We ought to see to it in our Christian experience that when we commit ourselves to God, the consequences will be all right. He who *"seeks to save his life will lose it, and whoever loses his life will preserve it"* (Luke 17:33).

What is it to be bound by the Almighty, preserved by the Infinite? There is no end to God's resources. They reach right into glory. They never finish on the earth. God takes control of a man in the baptism of the Holy Spirit as he yields himself to God. There is the possibility of being taken and yet left—taken charge of by God and left in the world to carry out His commands. That is one of God's possibilities for humanity: to be taken over by the power of God while being left in the world to be salt as the Scripture describes (Matt. 5:13).

A FRESH VISION FOR EACH DAY

Now, beloved, I am out to win souls. It is my business to seek the lost. It is my business to make everybody hungry, dissatisfied, mad, or glad. I want to see every person filled with the Holy Spirit. I must have a message from heaven that will not leave people as I found them. Something must happen if we are filled with the Holy Spirit. Something must happen at every place. Men must know that a man filled with the Holy Spirit is no longer a man. I told you when I was here last year that God has no room for ordinary men. A man can be swept by the power of God in his first stage of revelation of Christ, and from that moment on, he has to be an extraordinary man. In order to be filled with the Holy Spirit, he has to become a free body for God to dwell in. No man can have the Trinity abiding in him and be the same as he was before. I appeal to you who have been filled with the Holy Spirit, whatever the cost, let God have His way. I appeal to you people who have got to move on, who cannot rest until God does something for you. I appeal to you as I could never have appealed to you unless God had been speaking to me since I left this place. Let me tell you what He has been saying. God has been revealing to me that any man who does not sin yet remains in the same place spiritually for a week is a backslider. You say, "How is it possible?" Because God's revelation is available to anyone who will wholeheartedly be committed to following God.

Staying the same for two days would almost indicate that you had lost the vision. The child of God must have a fresh vision every day. The child of God must be more active by the Holy Spirit every day. The child of God must come into line with the power of heaven, where he knows that God has put His hand upon him. He must be able to say:

I know the Lord, I know the Lord,
 I know the Lord has laid His hand on me,
He filled me with the Holy Spirit.
 How do I know? Oh, the Spirit spoke through me.
I know the Lord has laid His hand on me,
 I know the Lord has laid His hand on me—Glory.
He healed the sick, and He raised the dead,
 I know the Lord has laid His hand on me.

Jesus went about doing good, for God was with Him. God anointed Him. Beloved, is that not the ministry to which God would have us become heir? Why? Because the Holy Spirit has to bring us a revelation of Jesus, and the purpose of being filled with the Holy Spirit is to give us a revelation of Jesus. He will make the Word of God just the same life as was given by the Son, as new, as fresh, as effective as if the Lord Himself were speaking.

I wonder how many of you are a part of the bride of Christ? The bride loves to hear the Bridegroom's voice (John 3:29). Here it is, the blessed Word of God, the whole Word, not just part of it. No, we believe in the whole thing. Day by day, we find out that the Word itself gives life. The Spirit of the Lord breathes through us. He makes the Word come alive in our hearts and minds. So I have within my hands, within my heart, within my mind, this blessed reservoir of promises that is able to do so many marvelous things.

I believe that the Lord will deliver some of the people in this meeting tonight. Some of you have most likely been suffering because you have a limited revelation of Jesus, a limited revelation of the fullness of Jesus, and there may be some who need to be delivered. I can see that we are surrounded by faith in a great way, differently from other places. Nevertheless, the Lord has been wonderfully manifesting Himself. Since I left you last year, I have seen wonderful things. God has indeed been manifesting Himself.

I must tell you one of those cases. In Oakland, California, I held meetings at a theater. Only to glorify God, I tell you that Oakland was in a very serious state. There was very little Pentecostal work there, and so a large theater was rented. God worked especially in filling the place until we had to have overflow meetings. In these meetings, we had a rising flood of people getting saved by rising up voluntarily, up and down the place, getting saved the moment they rose. Then we had a large number of people who needed help in their bodies, rising up in faith and being healed.

One of them was an old man who was ninety-five years of age. He had been suffering for three years until he gradually got to the place that for three weeks he was consuming only liquids. He was in a terrible state, but this man was different from the others. I got him to stand while I prayed for him, and he came back and told us with such a radiant face that new life had come into his body. He said, "I am ninety-five years old. When I came into the meeting, I was full of pain with cancer in the stomach. I have been healed so that I have been eating perfectly, and I have no pain." Similarly, many people were healed.

I believe that tonight God wants me to help some of you in this meeting. I want a manifestation to the glory of God. Anybody in this meeting who has pain in the head, in the feet, shoulders, or legs, if you want deliverance, rise up, and I will pray for you. You will find that God will so manifest His power that you will go out of this meeting free. If there is anyone in this meeting in pain, from the head to the feet, anywhere, if you will rise, I will pray for you, and the Lord will deliver you. I hope you are expecting big things.

If you look at Acts 2, you will find that the Holy Spirit came, and there was a manifestation of the divine power of God. It brought conviction as the Word was spoken in the Holy Spirit.

In Acts 3, we see that a man was healed at the Beautiful Gate, through the power of the Spirit. It was such a miraculous, wonderful evidence of the power of the Spirit that 5,000 men, women, and we don't know how many children, were saved by the power of God. God manifested His divine power to prove that He is with us.

Now, how many would like to give their hearts to God tonight? How many would like to be saved?

13

The Incarnation
of Man

especially want to speak to those who are saved. God wants you to be holy. He wants you to be filled with the power that will keep you holy. He wants you to have a revelation of what sin and death are, and what the Spirit and life of the Spirit are. Look at these two significant verses:

> *There is therefore now no condemnation to those who are in Christ Jesus, who do not walk according to the flesh, but according to the Spirit. For the law of the Spirit of life in Christ Jesus has made me free from the law of sin and death.* (Rom. 8:1–2)

"No condemnation." This is the primary thought for me because it means so much; it contains so much truth. If you are without condemnation, you are in a place where you can pray through. You can have a revelation of Christ. For Him to be in

you brings you to a place where you cannot, if you follow the definite leadings of the Spirit of Christ, have any fellowship with the world. I want you to see that the Spirit of the Lord would reveal this fact to us. If you love the world, you cannot love God, and the love of God cannot be in you (1 John 2:15). God wants a clear decision, because if you are in Christ Jesus, you are a *"new creation"* (2 Cor. 5:17). You are in Him; therefore, you walk in the Spirit and are free from condemnation.

An Interpretation of Tongues:

It is the Spirit alone that, by revelation, brings the whole truth, visiting the Son in your hearts, and reveals unto you the capabilities of sonship that are in you after you are created after the image of Him.

FREE FROM SIN

So the Spirit of the Lord would bring you into revelation. He wants you without condemnation. What will that mean? Much in every way, because God wants all His people to be clear witnesses so that the world will know we belong to God. More than that, He wants us to be *"the salt of the earth"* (Matt. 5:13); to be *"the light of the world"*(v. 14); to be like cities built on a hill so that they cannot be hidden (v. 14). He wants us to be so *"in God"* (1 John 4:15) that the world will see God in us. Then they can look to Him for redemption. That is the law of the Spirit. What will it do? *"The law of the Spirit of life in Christ Jesus"* will make you *"free from the law of sin and death"* (Rom. 8:2). Sin will have no dominion over you (Rom. 6:14). You will have no desire to sin, and it will be as true of you as it was of Jesus when He said, *"The ruler of this world is coming, and he has nothing in Me"* (John 14:30). Satan cannot influence; he has no power. His power is destroyed: *"The body is dead because of sin, but the Spirit is life because of righteousness"* (Rom. 8:10).

To be filled with God means that you are free. You are filled with joy, peace, blessing, and strength of character. You are transformed by God's mighty power.

Notice there are two laws. *"The law of the Spirit of life in Christ Jesus"* makes you *"free from the law of sin and death"* (v. 2). *"The law of sin and death"* is in you as it was before, but it is dead. You still have your same flesh, but its power over you is gone. You are the same person, but you have been awakened into spiritual life. You are a *"new creation"* (2 Cor. 5:17), created in God afresh after the image of Christ. Now, beloved, some people who conform to this truth do not understand their inheritance, and they go down. Instead of becoming weak, you have to rise triumphantly over *"the law of sin and death."* In Romans, we read: *"I thank God; through Jesus Christ our Lord! So then, with the mind I myself serve the law of God, but with the flesh the law of sin"* (7:25).

God wants to show you that there is a place where we can live in the Spirit and not be subject to the flesh. We can live in the Spirit until sin has no dominion over us. We reign in life and see the covering of God over us in the Spirit. Sin reigned unto death, but Christ reigned over sin and death, and so we reign with Him in life.

Not a sick person here could be said to be reigning in life. Satanic power reigns there, and God wants you to know that you have to reign. God made you like Himself, and in the Garden of Gethsemane, Jesus restored to you everything that was lost in the Garden of Eden. Through the agony He suffered, He purchased our blessed redemption.

OUR GLORIOUS REDEMPTION

People say, "Could anything be greater than the fellowship that prevailed in the Garden of Eden when God walked and talked and had fellowship with man?" Yes, redemption is greater. Nothing but what was local was in the garden, but the moment a man is born again, he is free from the world and lives in heavenly places. He has no destination except heaven.

Redemption is, therefore, greater than the Garden of Eden, and God wants you to know that you may receive this glorious redemption not only for salvation, but also for the restoration of your bodies. They are redeemed from the curse of the law. You have been made free, and all praise and glory are due the Son of God. Hallelujah! No more Egypt places! No more sandy deserts! Praise the Lord! Free *"from the law of sin and death"* (Rom. 8:2). How was it accomplished? These verses from Romans answer that question. Pay particular attention to verse three. It contains the supreme truth:

> *For what the law could not do in that it was weak through the flesh, God did by sending His own Son in the likeness of sinful flesh, on*

account of sin: He condemned sin in the flesh,
that the righteous requirement of the law
might be fulfilled in us who do not walk ac-
cording to the flesh but according to the Spirit.
(Rom. 8:3–4)

Righteousness was fulfilled in us! Brother and sister, I tell you there is a redemption. There is an atonement in Christ. There is a personality of Christ to dwell in you. There is a Godlikeness for you to attain, a blessed resemblance to Christ. The God in you will not fail if you believe the Word of God.

An Interpretation of Tongues:
The living Word is sufficient for you. Eat it. Devour it. It is the Word of God.

FILLED WITH GOD

Jesus came to destroy the works of the Devil. God was manifested in Him. The fullness of God resided in Jesus, and He walked about glorified, filled with God. Incarnate! May I embody Christ? Yes. How can I be so filled with God that all my movements, my desires, my mind, and my will are so controlled by a new power that I no longer exist, for God has filled me? Praise the Lord! Certainly it can be so. Did you ever examine the condition of your new birth into righteousness? Did you ever investigate it? Did you ever try to see what there was in it? Were you ever able to fathom the fullness of redemption that came to you through believing in Jesus?

Before *"the foundation of the world,"* redemption was all completed (Matt. 25:34). It was set in order before the Fall. This redemption had to be so mighty and had to redeem us all so perfectly that there would be no deficiency in the whole of redemption.

Let us see how it came about: *"In the beginning was the Word, and the Word was with God, and the Word was God"* (John 1:1). He became flesh. Then, He became the voice and the operation of the Word. By the power of God through the Holy Spirit, He became the Authority. Now, let me go further with you.

BORN OF GOD

You are born of an incorruptible power of God (1 Pet. 1:23), born of the Word, who has the personality and nature of God. You were begotten of God, and *"you are not your own"* (1 Cor. 6:19). You can believe that you have *"passed from death into life"* (John 5:24) and have become *"heirs of God and joint heirs with Christ"* (Rom. 8:17) in the measure in which you believe His Word. The natural flesh, the first order, has been changed into a new order, for the first order was Adam, the natural, and the last order was Christ, the heavenly. Now you have been changed by a heavenly power existing in an earthly body, and that power can never die. I want you to see that you are born of a power and have existing in you the power that God used to create the world. It is *"the law of the Spirit of life in Christ Jesus"* that makes you *"free from the law of sin and death"* (v. 2).

Now, let us look at the law without the Spirit, *"the law of sin and death."* Here is a man who has never come into the new law. He is still in the law of Adam, never having been regenerated, never having been born again. He is led captive by the Devil at his will. There is no power that can convert a man except the power of the blood of Jesus. The carnal mind is *"not subject to the law of God, nor indeed can be"* (Rom. 8:7). Carnality is selfishness and uncleanness. It cannot be subject to God. It interferes with you by binding you and keeping you in bondage. But God destroys carnality by a new life, which is so much better, and fills you *"with joy inexpressible and full of glory"* (1 Pet. 1:8). The half can never be told. Everything that God does is too big to tell. His grace, His love, His mercy, and His salvation are all too big to understand.

Do you not know that ours is an abundant God, *"who is able to do exceedingly abundantly above all that we ask or think"* (Eph. 3:20)? We are illuminated and quickened by the Spirit, looking forward to the Rapture when we will be caught up and lifted into the presence of God. God's boundaries are enormous, wonderful, and glorious!

A RISEN SAVIOR

Now, let me touch on another important point. Can you think about Jesus being dead in the grave? Do you think that God could do anything for us if Jesus were still there? After His crucifixion and until He was laid in the grave, everything had to be done for Him, and I want you to see that a dead Christ can do nothing for you. He carried the cross, so don't you carry it. The Cross covered everything, and the Resurrection brought everything to life. When He was in the grave, the Word of God says that He was raised by the operation of God through the Spirit. Jesus was awakened by the Spirit in the grave, and this same Spirit dwells in your mortal bodies. Jesus rose by the quickening power of the Holy Spirit:

> *But if the Spirit of Him who raised Jesus from the dead dwells in you, He who raised Christ from the dead will also give life to your mortal bodies through His Spirit who dwells in you.*
> (Rom. 8:11)

If you will allow Jesus to have charge of your bodies, you will find that this Spirit will quicken you and will free you. Talk about divine healing! You cannot remove it from the Scriptures. They are full of it. You will find, also, that all who are healed by the power of God, especially believers, will find their healing an incentive to make them purer and holier. If divine healing merely made the body whole, it would be worth very little. Divine healing is the marvelous act of the providence of God coming into your mortal bodies, and after being touched by the Almighty, can you ever remain the same? No. Like me, you will eagerly worship and serve God.

14

Filled with God

You may be filled
with all the fullness of God.
—Ephesians 3:19

ome people come with very small expectations concerning God's fullness, and a lot
of people are satisfied with a thimbleful.
You can just imagine God saying, "Oh, if
they only knew how much they could take away!"
Other people come with a larger container, and they
go away satisfied. God is longing for us to have such
a desire for more, a desire that only He can satisfy.

You women would have a good idea of what I
mean from the illustration of a screaming child being
passed from one person to another. The child is never
satisfied until he gets to the arms of his mother. You
will find that no peace, no help, no source of strength,
no power, no life, nothing can satisfy the cry of the
child of God but the Word of God. God has a special
way of satisfying the cries of His children. He is
waiting to open the windows of heaven until He has
moved in the depths of our hearts so that everything
unlike Himself has been destroyed. No one needs to

go away empty. God wants you to be filled. My brother, my sister, God wants you today to be like a watered garden, filled with the fragrance of His own heavenly joy, until you know at last that you have touched the immense fullness of God. The Son of God came for no other purpose than to lift, to mold, and to remold, until *"we have the mind of Christ"* (1 Cor. 2:16).

ASK LARGELY OF GOD

I know that dry ground can be flooded (Isa. 44:3). May God prevent me from ever wanting anything less than a flood. I will not settle for small things when I have such a big God. Through the blood of Christ's atonement, we may have riches and riches. We need the warming atmosphere of the Spirit's power to bring us closer and closer until nothing but God can satisfy. Then we may have some idea of what God has left after we have taken all that we can. It is like a sparrow taking a drink of the ocean and then looking around and saying, "What a vast ocean! What a lot more I could have taken if I only had room."

Sometimes you have things you can use, and you don't know it. You could be dying of thirst right in a river of plenty. There was once a boat in the mouth of the Amazon River. The people on board thought they were still in the ocean. They were dying of thirst, some of them nearly mad. They saw a ship and asked if they would give them some water. Someone on the ship replied, "Dip your bucket right over; you are in the mouth of the river." There are a number of people today in the middle of the great river of life, but they are dying of thirst because they do not dip down and take from the river. Dear friend, you may have the Word, but you need an awakened spirit. The Word is not alive until it is moved upon by the Spirit of God, and in the right sense, it becomes Spirit and Life when it is touched by His hand alone.

Beloved, *"there is a river whose streams shall make glad the city of God, the holy place of the tabernacle of the Most High"* (Ps. 46:4). There is a stream of life that makes everything move. There is a touch of divine life and likeness through the Word of God that comes from nowhere else. We think of death as the absence of life, but there is a death-likeness in Christ, which is full of life.

There is no such thing as an end to God's beginnings. We must be in Christ; we must know Him. Life in Christ is not a touch; it is not a breath; it is the almighty God; it is a Person; it is the Holy One dwelling in the temple *"not made with hands"* (Heb. 9:11). Oh, beloved, He touches, and it is done. He is the same God over all, *"rich to all who call upon Him"* (Rom. 10:12). Pentecost is the last thing that God has to touch the earth with. If you do not receive the baptism of the Holy Spirit, you are living in a weak and impoverished condition, which is no good to yourself or anybody else. May God move us on to a place where there is no measure to this fullness that He wants to give us. God exalted Jesus and gave Him a name above every name. You notice that everything has been put under Him.

It has been about eight years since I was in Oakland, California, and since that time, I have seen thousands and thousands healed by the power of God. In the last five months of the year, we had over 7,000 people in Sweden saved by the power of God. The tide is rolling in. Let us see to it today that we get right into the tide, for it will hold us. God's heart of love is the center of all things. Get your eyes off yourself; lift them up high, and see the Lord, for in Him, there *"is everlasting strength"* (Isa. 26:4).

If you went to see a doctor, the more you told him about yourself, the more he would know. But when you come to Doctor Jesus, He knows all from the beginning, and He never prescribes the wrong medicine. Jesus sends His healing power and brings His restoring grace, so there is nothing to fear. The only thing that is wrong is your wrong conception of His redemption.

Take Authority over Satan

He was wounded that He might be able to identify with your weaknesses (Heb. 4:15). He took your flesh and laid it upon the cross that *"He might destroy him who had the power of death, that is, the devil, and release those who through fear of death were all their lifetime subject to bondage"* (Heb. 2:14–15).

You will find that almost all the ailments that you experience come as a result of Satan, and they must be dealt with as satanic; they must be cast out. Do not listen to what Satan says to you, for the Devil is a liar from the beginning (John 8:44). If people would only listen to the truth of God, they would realize that every evil spirit is subject to them. They would find out that they are always in the place of triumph, and they would *"reign in life through the One, Jesus Christ"* (Rom. 5:17).

Never live in a place other than where God has called you, and He has called you from on high to live with Him. God has designed that everything will be subject to man. Through Christ, He has given you authority over all the power of the Enemy. He has worked out your eternal redemption.

I was finishing a meeting one day in Switzerland. When the meeting ended and we had ministered to all the sick, we went out to see some people. Two boys came to us and said that there was a blind man present at the meeting that afternoon. He had heard all the words of the preacher and said he was surprised that he had not been prayed for. They went on to say that this blind man had heard so much that he would not leave until he could see. I said, "This is positively unique. God will do something today for that man."

We got to the place. The blind man said he had never seen. He was born blind, but because of the Word preached in the afternoon, he was not going home until he could see. If ever I have joy, it is when I have a lot of people who will not be satisfied until they get all that they have come for. With great joy, I anointed him and laid hands on his eyes. Immediately, God restored his vision. It was very strange how the man reacted. There were some electric lights. First he counted them; then he counted us. Oh, the ecstatic pleasure that this man experienced every moment because of his sight! It made us all feel like weeping and dancing and shouting. Then he pulled out his watch and said that for years he had been feeling the raised figures on the watch in order to tell the time. But now, he could look at it and tell us the time. Then, looking as if he had just awakened from some deep sleep, or some long, strange dream, he realized that he had never seen the faces of his father and mother. He went to the door and rushed out. That night, he was the first person to arrive for the meeting. All the people knew him as the blind man, and I had to give him a long time to talk about his new sight.

I wonder how much you want to take away today. You could not carry it if it were substance, but there is something about the grace, the power, and the blessings of God that can be carried, no matter how big they are. Oh, what a Savior. What a place we are in, by grace, that He may come in to commune with us. He is willing to say to every heart, *"Peace, be still"* (Mark 4:39), and to every weak body, *"Be strong"* (Deut. 31:6).

Are you going halfway, or are you going all the way to the end? Do not be deceived by Satan, but believe God.

15

Joint Heirs with Christ

I used to have a hard heart, and God had to completely break me. I used to be critical of people who preached divine healing and did certain things that I thought they should not do. Then God began to put me through a testing and to subdue me. I fell down before God, and then the hardness and all the bitterness were taken away. I believe God wants to remove the critical sprit from us. He wants to replace it with His Spirit. As the Scripture says:

> But if the Spirit of Him who raised Jesus from
> the dead dwells in you, He who raised Christ
> from the dead will also give life to your mortal
> bodies through His Spirit who dwells in you.
> (Rom. 8:11)

Here the power of God is dealing with our *"mortal bodies,"* but the power of the Spirit today wants to revive us both in spirit and body:

> For if you live according to the flesh you will
> die; but if by the Spirit you put to death the

deeds of the body, you will live. For as many as are led by the Spirit of God, these are sons of God. For you did not receive the spirit of bondage again to fear, but you received the Spirit of adoption by whom we cry out, "Abba, Father." The Spirit Himself bears witness with our spirit that we are children of God, and if children, then heirs; heirs of God and joint heirs with Christ, if indeed we suffer with Him, that we may also be glorified to-gether. (vv. 13–17)

THE PRIVILEGES OF ADOPTION

The thought that especially comes to me today is that of our relationship to our heavenly Father. The Spirit brings us to a place where we see that we are children of God. And because of this glorious posi-tion, we are not only children but heirs, and not only heirs, but joint heirs. Because of that, *"all the prom-ises of God in Him are Yes, and...Amen"* (2 Cor. 1:20). If the Spirit of God *"who raised Jesus from the dead dwells in you, He who raised Christ from the dead will also give life to your mortal bodies through His Spirit who dwells in you"* (Rom. 8:11).

It brings me into a living place to believe that as an adopted child, I may grasp the promises. I see two wonderful things: I see deliverance for the body, and I see the power of the Spirit in sonship raising me up and pressing me onward to resurrection through faith in the Lord Jesus Christ. That promise is found in His Word:

Jesus spoke these words, lifted up His eyes to heaven, and said: "Father, the hour has come.

Joint Heirs with Christ

Glorify Your Son, that Your Son also may glo-
rify You, as You have given Him authority
over all flesh, that He should give eternal life
to as many as You have given Him. And this is
eternal life, that they may know You, the only
true God, and Jesus Christ whom You have
sent." (John 17:1–3)

It is no small thing to be brought into fellowship with the Father through Jesus Christ. The Spirit that is in you not only puts to death all other power, but He is showing us our privilege and bringing us into a faith where we can claim all we need. The moment a man comes into the knowledge of Christ, he is made an heir of heaven. By the Spirit, he is being changed into the image of the Son of God. It is in that image that we can definitely look into the face of the Father and see that the things we ask for are done: *"And if children, then heirs; heirs of God and joint heirs with Christ, if indeed we suffer with Him, that we may also be glorified together"* (Rom. 8:17).

And the glory is not only going to be revealed, but it is already revealed in us. We are being changed *"from glory to glory"* (2 Cor. 3:18). I want you to know what it means to be children of God. I want you to know that the Spirit that raised Jesus from the dead is dwelling in your mortal body, making you His child. *"We shall be like Him, for we shall see Him as He is"* (1 John 3:2). It does not mean that we will have faces like Jesus, but we will have the same Spirit. When they look at us and see the glory, they will say, "Yes, it is the same Spirit," for they will see the radiance of the glory of Jesus

Christ. Beloved, we are being changed: *"For the earnest expectation of the creation eagerly waits for the revealing of the sons of God"* (Rom. 8:19).

All of us who are born of God and have the power of the Holy Spirit within are longing for the evidence of our adoption. You say, when will these things happen? Paul, in a spirit of expectation, writes:

> *For we know that the whole creation groans and labors with birth pangs together until now. Not only that, but we also who have the firstfruits of the Spirit, even we ourselves groan within ourselves, eagerly waiting for the adoption, the redemption of our body.*
>
> (vv. 22–23)

WAITING FOR DELIVERANCE

Within me this afternoon, there is a cry and a longing for deliverance. Praise God, it is coming! There is a true sense even now in which you may live in the resurrection power. The Holy Spirit is working in us and bringing us to a condition where we know He is doing a work in us. I never felt so near heaven as last night when the house was shaking with an earthquake, and I thought my Lord might come. More than crossing the sea and seeing my children, I would rather see Jesus. Praise God, we are delivered by the power of the Spirit: *"Because the creation itself also will be delivered from the bondage of corruption into the glorious liberty of the children of God"* (v. 21).

Do not ask how can this be. The sovereign grace and power of God are equal to all these things. I have been changed by the power of the Holy Spirit, and I know that there is a better man in me than the natural man.

Brothers and sisters, are you really *"waiting for the adoption"* (v. 23)? The baptism of the Holy Spirit links heaven to earth, and God wants us to be so filled with the Spirit and walk in the Spirit so that while we live here on earth, our heads will be right up in heaven. Brothers and sisters, the Spirit can give you patience to wait. The baptism in the Holy Spirit is the essential power in the body that will bring rest from all your weariness and give you a hopeful expectation that each day may be the day we go up with Him. We must not be foolish people, folding our hands and giving up everything. I find there is no time like the present to be up and active. We need our bodies to be strengthened by the Spirit; otherwise, we would be entirely worn-out. The Holy Spirit Himself will pray through you and help you to remember the things for which you should pray, for *"the Spirit also helps in our weaknesses"* (v. 26). Is there anyone who could say, "I have no need for the Holy Spirit"?

THE NEED FOR TRANSFORMATION

The highest purpose God has for us is that we will be transformed into the image of His Son. We have seen in part God's purpose in filling us with the Spirit that He might conform us to the image of His Son. Paul writes:

> *For whom He foreknew, He also predestined to be conformed to the image of His Son, that He*

might be the firstborn among many brethren. Moreover whom He predestined, these He also called; whom He called, these He also justified; and whom He justified, these He also glorified. (Rom. 8:29–30)

Where are you standing? I believe there are two kinds of people: the whosoever will and the whosoever won't. I want you to examine yourselves to see where you stand. If you stand on these truths that God has given, you will be amazed to see how God will make everything happen so that you will be conformed to the image of His Son.

It is a sad thing today to see how people are astonished at the workings of God. Millions of years ago He purposed in His heart to do this mighty thing in us. Are you going to refuse it, or are you going to yield? I thank God He planned ahead for me to be saved. Some will receive Christ, but others will not believe in Him for salvation. You see it is a mystery, but God purposed it *"before the foundation of the world"* (Eph. 1:4). And if you yield, He will put in you a living faith, and you cannot get away from the power of it. Oh, brothers and sisters, let us come a little nearer. How amazing it is that we can be transformed so that the thoughts of Christ will be first in our minds. How blessed that when everybody around you is interested in everything else, you are thinking about Jesus Christ.

WHAT IS YOUR RESPONSE?

Friends, it is the purpose of God that you should rise into the place of sonship. Don't miss the purpose

God has in His heart for you. Realize that God wants to make of you the firstfruits (James 1:18) and separate you unto Himself. God has lifted some of you up again and again. It is amazing how God in His mercy has restored and restored, and *"whom He called, these He also justified; and whom He justified, these He also glorified"* (Rom. 8:30). The glorification is still going on and is going to exceed what it is now.

Within your heart there surely must be a response to this call. It does not matter who is against us: *"What then shall we say to these things? If God is for us, who can be against us?"* (v. 31). If there are millions against you, God has purposed it and will bring you right through to glory. Human wisdom has to stand still. It is *"with the heart one believes unto righteousness"* (Rom. 10:10).

Brothers and sisters, what do you want? That is the question. What have you come here for? We have seen God work in horribly diseased bodies. Our God is able to heal and to meet all of our needs. The Scripture says: *"He who did not spare His own Son, but delivered Him up for us all, how shall He not with Him also freely give us all things?"* (Rom. 8:32).

Do you need to be healed of a critical spirit? The Scripture warns: *"Who shall bring a charge against God's elect?"* (v. 33). I tell you, it is bad business for the man who harms God's anointed (1 Chron. 16:21–22). *"Who is he who condemns?"* (Rom. 8:34). How much of that there is today: brother condemning brother, everybody condemning one another. You also go about condemning yourself. The Devil is the *"accuser of* [the] *brethren"* (Rev. 12:10). But there is power in the blood to free us, to keep us, and to bring us healing.

Do not let the Enemy cripple you and bind you. Why don't you believe God's Word? There is a blessed place for you in the Holy Spirit. Instead of condemning you, Christ is interceding for you. Rest in this promise:

> *For I am persuaded that neither death nor life, nor angels nor principalities nor powers, nor things present nor things to come, nor height nor depth, nor any other created thing, shall be able to separate us from the love of God which is in Christ Jesus our Lord.* (Rom. 8:38–39)

Beloved, you are in a wonderful place. Because God has called and chosen you, He wants you to know that you have power with Him. Because you are sons and joint heirs, you have a right to healing for your bodies and to be delivered from all the power of the Enemy.

16

Apprehend Your Apprehension

Read Philippians 3. It contains wonderful words that encourage us to be filled with all the fullness of God. God's Word is our food. If we do not edify ourselves with it, our needs will not be met. Let us preach by our lives, actions, presence, and praise, always being living letters of Christ. We should strive to be examples to all men of the truth contained in the Word of God.

Follow the truth, and do not abandon it. Always be watchful for divine inspiration. If we were to go all the way with God, what would happen? Seek the honor that comes from God alone. Paul speaks about the desire to attain. He says that he reached for *"the goal for the prize of the upward call of God in Christ Jesus"* (Phil. 3:14). There is no standing still. We are renewed by the Spirit. Although we are always striving for more of God, we have a sense of contentment in Him.

FOLLOW GOD'S COMMAND

Abraham left his home and followed God to a new land (Gen. 12:1–4). We never get into a new place until we come out of the old one. We must model God's personality. We can never be satisfied to stay where we are spiritually, for the truth continues to enlighten us. We must move on, or we will perish. We must be obedient to the Holy Spirit who guides us.

Paul was a man who had kept the law blamelessly. He had tried in his humanity to follow an ideal standard. Then Paul saw a light from heaven, and he was made new. Are you new? He was not with the other apostles, but he had been told of *"the Word of life"* (1 John 1:1). He had not yet attained to these ideal principles, but he had zeal. Before him was a challenge. He was to *"go into the city"* (Acts 9:6) where he would be told what to do. The present was nothing to him; he was motivated to follow God's command. Everything that had been important to him before, he now counted *"loss for the excellence of the knowledge of Christ Jesus* [his] *Lord"* (Phil. 3:8). His chief goal was to *"gain Christ"* (v. 8).

When Judas and the soldiers came after Jesus in the garden, Jesus spoke, and the men fell backward (John 18:6). He, the Creator, submitted Himself to these men. Yet He said, *"Let these go their way"* (v. 8), referring to the disciples. When they abused Him, He did not retaliate. Paul understood these Christlike principles. He recognized the power of Christ, which is able to lift our humanity.

JESUS IS OUR EXAMPLE

Jesus' followers sought to make Him a King, but Jesus retired to pray. Paul desired to *"gain Christ and be found in Him"* (Phil. 3:8–9). Oh, can I gain

Him? Is it possible to change and change, having His compassion, His love?

In an effort to prevent Jesus from being taken, Peter cut off Malchus's ear (John 18:10). Jesus put it on again. See the dignity of Christ, who comes to create a new order of life. May we *"gain Christ and be found in Him"* that we might have the *"right-eousness which is from God by faith"* (Phil. 3:8–9).

Jesus identified Himself with us. He came to be a firstfruit (1 Cor. 15:23). How zealous is the farmer as he watches his crops to see the first shoots and blades of the harvest. Jesus was a firstfruit, and God will have a harvest! What a lovely position to be children of God, perfectly adjusted in the presence of God and *"found in Him"* (Phil. 3:9)! You say, "It is a trying morning," or "I am in a needy place." He knows and understands your needs. When Jesus saw a great crowd coming toward Him, He said to Philip, *"Where shall we buy bread, that these may eat?"* (John 6:5). Jesus knew where the food would come from. He was testing Philip's faith. From a little boy's lunch, Jesus fed over five thousand. They were all filled, and twelve baskets of bread were left over (v. 13).

HE IS HERE

Did you ever walk a while on the way to Em-maus? The two who walked with Jesus thought He was a stranger. If we only knew that He is by our sides! He made Himself known to them in the break-ing of the bread (Luke 24:30–31). The same day, He appeared again and said, *"Peace to you"* (v. 36). Oh, to be found in the place where He is! How did He get there? He was there all the time. We need to have our eyes open. He is always there to bring us to the place where we are confident; the Lord is with us. There is such a place. Abraham walked there. Jesus lived it. Paul desired it. Have you got it?

"Found in Him" (Phil. 3:9). It is there where we can receive *"the righteousness which is from God by faith"* (v. 9). Abraham received it. God gave him righteousness because he believed, and God credited him with righteousness. God adds in order to take away. He takes away hindrances and imparts the biggest blessing: the rest of faith. God *"will keep him in perfect peace, whose mind is stayed on* [Him]*"* (Isa. 26:3).

EXPERIENCE HIS RESURRECTION POWER

Jesus had what Paul desired. Paul knew Jesus by revelation as we do. He did not know Him from being with Him in His human ministry as the other apostles did. Paul saw that Jesus lived in resurrection power. Paul wanted to gain the rest of faith, so he refused all hindrances and pressed on. He wanted to remove any interference that stood in the way of his knowing Christ. Before facing the Cross, Jesus told His disciples to *"stay here and watch"* (Mark 14:34) while He went further in the garden to pray. Jesus went to the place of apprehension to attain. We also must watch and pray if we are to *"know Him and the power of His resurrection"* (Phil. 3:10).

One day Jesus came upon a funeral procession. A widow's only son had died, and Jesus' great heart had compassion for her. He touched her son in his coffin and said, *"Young man, I say to you, arise"*

(Luke 7:14). Death had no power; it could not hold him: *"He who was dead sat up and began to speak"* (v. 15). Oh, compassion is greater than death, greater than suffering. Oh, God, give it to us.

One day, I saw a woman with tumors. In the condition she was in, she could not live out that day. I said, "Do you want to live?" She could not speak, but she was able to move her finger. In the name of Jesus, I anointed her with oil. Mr. Fisher, who was with me, said, "She's gone!"

It had been a little blind girl who had led me to this dying mother's bedside. Compassion broke my heart for that child. I had said to the mother, "Lift your finger." Carrying the mother across the room, I put her against the wardrobe. I held her there. I said, "In the name of Jesus, death, come out." Like a fallen tree, leaf after leaf, her body began moving. Upright instead of lifeless, her feet touched the floor. "In Jesus' name, walk," I said. She did, back to her bed.

I told this story in the service. There was a doctor there who said, "I'll prove that." He saw her and confirmed that the story was true. She told the doctor: "It is all true. I was in heaven, and I saw countless numbers all like Jesus. He pointed, and I knew I had to go. Then I heard a voice saying, 'Walk, in the name of Jesus.'"

There is power in His resurrection. There is a *"righteousness which is from God by faith"* (Phil. 3:9). Are we able to comprehend it? Can we have it? It is His love. It is His life in us. It is His compassion.

See that apprehension is apprehended. Miss it not. Oh, miss Him not! It is the *"righteousness which is from God by faith"*—the rest of faith.

17

Sonship

*Behold what manner of love the Father
has bestowed on us, that we should be called
children of God! Therefore the world does not know
us, because it did not know Him. Beloved, now we
are children of God.*
—1 John 3:1–2

God has done something marvelous for the believer. He has taken him out of the world. It is a remarkable word that Jesus said: *"I do not pray that You should take them out of the world....They are not of the world"* (John 17:15–16). It is a great truth for us to understand. In this glorious position of God's own, we come to a place where we know with confidence, we say it without fear of contradiction from our own hearts or even outside voices, *"Beloved, now we are children of God."*

I want us to examine ourselves in the light of the Word. God has definitely purposed that we should inherit all of the Scriptures, but we must meet the requirements necessary to claim them.

Remember this, there are any number of things you may quote without possessing the essential reality of them. I want us to have something more than the literal word. Words are of no importance unless the believer has the assurance of the abiding of those words.

Let me say a few things that are contained in the Scriptures that should be ours. Here is one: *"Beloved, now we are children of God."* That is Scripture. That is divine. That is for us, but it is another thing altogether to have it. Here is another word: *"He who practices righteousness is righteous, just as He is righteous"* (1 John 3:7). There is another word I want to give you. It is a verse that is used by most believers: *"He who is in you is greater than he who is in the world"* (1 John 4:4). That is quoted by many people, but may God reveal to us that the meaning is more than just saying it. You can quote these words without being in the place of victory.

Any person who has come to the place of this word, *"He who is in you is greater than he who is in the world,"* is mightier than all the powers of darkness, mightier than the power of disease, mightier than his own self. There is something reigning supremely great in him more than in the world when he is in that place. But we must come to the place of knowledge. It is not sufficient for you to quote the Word of God. You never come to a place of righteousness and truth until you are in possession of the promises contained in the Word.

An Interpretation of Tongues:
God, who has divinely brought forth the Word
by the power of His might through His Son,

gave it displacement in the human soul that the human may be dried up, withered by God, coming in by the force of living power.

Beloved, God wants us to be something more than ordinary people. Remember this: if you are ordinary, you have not reached the ideal principles of God. The only thing that God has for a man is to be extraordinary. God has no room for an ordinary man. There are millions of ordinary people in the world. But when God takes hold of a man, He makes him extraordinary in personality, power, thought, and activity.

"Beloved, now we are children of God." It is a divine plan fashioned by His divine will. God has not given anything that He does not mean for us to attain. God means for us to possess all these things. *"Beloved, now we are children of God."* God has such purposes to perform in us that He has a great desire to utter these words in our hearts that we may rise, that we may claim, that we may be ambitious, that we may be covetous, that there may be something in us that nothing can satisfy unless we not only tow the line but live in the line and claim the whole thing as ours.

You will never reach ideal purposes in any way unless you become the living epistle of the Word by the power of the Holy Spirit. You become the living force of the revelation of God, the incarnation of the personality of His presence in the human soul. Then you know that you are His children. Look at Christ. He is the most beautiful of all. He is utterly glorious, passionate for God, filled with all the fullness of God. He came to earth in the glory of the majesty of

His Father, and He stood in the earth in human form. Read Romans 8:3 with me. It is a good word to concentrate on:

> *For what the law could not do in that it was weak through the flesh, God did by sending His own Son in the likeness of sinful flesh, on account of sin: He condemned sin in the flesh.*

Jesus came in human form, *"born of a woman"* (Gal. 4:4), and took on the weaknesses of human flesh. Look at Hebrews 2:14, for there will be a blessing for you:

> *Inasmuch then as the children have partaken of flesh and blood, He Himself likewise shared in the same; that through death He might destroy him who had the power of death, that is, the devil.*

I like to think about the manifestation of the power of God. God came and resided in flesh, in weakness, under the law—for you. He came in human form, worshipped in it, lived in it, and moved in it. They recognized Him as the Son of God.

An Interpretation of Tongues:
Yes, it was the purpose of the Almighty to move through weakness and quicken it by His mighty power until flesh became the habitation of God in the Spirit.

Beloved, there is the principle. The remarkable position of every soul is to be so inhabited by Jesus as to become a living personality of God's ideal Son. It is very remarkable and beautiful. God has these divine plans for us because so many people believe that because they are in the flesh that they are always to be in the place of weakness. Friends, your weaknesses have to be swallowed up with the ideal of Him who never failed.

Every time He was tried, He came out victorious. He *"was in all points tempted as we are, yet without sin"* (Heb. 4:15). The purpose for His temptations was so that He might be able to help all who are tempted and tried and oppressed in any way. He was the great embodiment of God to human life. He came to expose our weaknesses that we might behold His mightiness. Through Him, we can be strong in the Lord. Praise the Lord!

> It's all right now, it's all right now,
> For Jesus is my Savior and it's all right now.

It is always all right when He is almighty. Then we are all right. The Word of God says:

> *Therefore, having been justified by faith, we have peace with God through our Lord Jesus Christ, through whom also we have access by faith into this grace in which we stand, and rejoice in hope of the glory of God.*
>
> (Rom. 5:1–2)

It is a great position to be saved by this immensity of power, this great inflow of life, this great fullness of God. This wonderful inhabiting of the Spirit comes right into the human soul and shakes the husks away, shakes the mind!

DIVINELY ADJUSTED

Many people have lost out because their minds prevent them from letting God reach their hearts. May God show us that the only thing that is ever going to help us is the heart. *"For with the heart one believes unto righteousness"* (Rom. 10:10). It is the heart where we believe in faith. It is the heart that is inhabited by the Spirit. It is the heart that is moved by God. The mind is always secondary.

The heart conceives, the mind reflects, and the mouth is operated. But you must not try to reverse the order. Some people are all tongue, neither head nor heart. But when He comes, there is perfect order. It is as right as rain. Look how it comes! The heart believes and then like a ventilator, it flows through and quickens the members of the mind. Then the tongue speaks of the glory of the Lord.

An Interpretation of Tongues:

Oh, it was the love that flowed from Calvary that moved with compassion for the mighty need of the world's cry. It entered the heart of the Father, unveiled His love to the world, gave us His Son in affection, and the work was done.

Praise the Lord! Then it is done. It is perfectly done. The Scriptures are perfect, the sacrifice is perfect, the revelation is perfect, and everything is so divinely adjusted by God Almighty that every person who comes into infinite revelation touched by God sees that the whole canon of Scripture is perfect from the beginning to the end. Not a single thing in the Scriptures clashes with or contradicts the Spirit and makes trouble.

When the power of God surges through the whole life, the Word becomes the personality of the subject. We become the subjects of the Spirit of the living God, and we are moved by the power of God until *"we live and move and have our being"* (Acts 17:28) within this flow of God's integrity. What a wonderful adjustment for weaknesses! Do you believe it is possible?

"God is able to make all grace abound" (2 Cor. 9:8). God is able to shake us thoroughly, to send a wind and blow the chaff away until it will never be seen anymore. God is able to refine us in a way that everyone would desire to proclaim His praises:

> It is better to shout than to doubt,
>   It is better to rise than to fail,
> It is better to let the glory out,
>   Than to have no glory at all.

"Beloved, now we are children of God." I don't want to leave the subject until I feel that God has given you the hope and ability to bring you into the very place He has made for you. It is as easy as possible if you can reach out by faith.

I am the last man to say anything about fasting, praying, or anything that has been a source of blessing to others. But I have learned by personal experience that I can get more out of one moment's faith than I can get out of a month's yelling. I can get more by believing God in a moment than I can get by screaming for a month. Also, I am positive that blessing comes out of fasting when the fasting is done in the right way. But I find so many people who make up their minds to fast, and they finish with a thick head, troubled bones, and sleepy conditions. I am satisfied that that is no way to fast. A way to fast is described in many Scriptures.

Praying and fasting go together. The Spirit leads you to pray. The Spirit holds on to you until you forget even the hour or the day, and you are so caught up by the power of the Spirit that you want nothing, not even food or drink. Then God gets His plan through because He has you through and through. So the Lord of Hosts, I trust, will *"surround* [us] *with songs of deliverance"* (Ps. 32:7) and give us inward revelations until our whole beings will be uplifted.

Now I can understand clearer than ever Psalm 24: *"Lift up your heads, O you gates!"* (v. 7). Human gates, human hindrances, human thoughts, and human trying can block the Spirit. *"Lift up your heads, O you gates! And be lifted up, you everlasting doors! And the King of glory shall come in"* (v. 7). Let Him in! Oh, if He comes in, what a wonderful Jesus! You say, "He is in." I believe that when you let God in, you gladly give Him full possession of your heart. The difficulty is that some people are on the edge, waiting to see which way to go. Friends, that is a dangerous position to be in. May God the Holy Spirit wake us up to see we must rise to the challenge of His call.

Who dares to believe God? Who dares to claim his rights? What are your rights? *"Now we are children of God."* This is a position of absolute rest, a position of faith. It is a place of perfect trust and perfect habitation where there are no disturbances. You experience peace like a river. Look at the face of God. Hallelujah! The very Word that comes to judge comes to help.

The law came as a judgment, but when the Spirit comes and breathes through the law, He comes to lift us higher and higher. Hallelujah! We must go a little further. God comes to us and says, "I will make it all right if you dare believe."

All the great things of God come to us as we realize our sinfulness before Him. Instead of hiding as Adam and Eve did when they realized they were naked (Gen. 3:7–10), we should come to God to be clothed. We cannot associate with the evil of this world. If you can be attracted by anything earthly, you have missed the greatest association that God has for you. If your property, your money, your friends, or any human thing can attract you from God, you are not His child in this respect. I will prove it by the next words:

> *Beloved, now we are children of God; and it has not yet been revealed what we shall be, but we know that when He is revealed, we shall be like Him, for we shall see Him as He is. And everyone who has this hope in Him purifies himself, just as He is pure.* (1 John 3:2–3)

Hallelujah! So you see, beloved, the importance of coming into line with God's Word. Let us encounter the Word; let us face God and see if this thing really is so.

ASSOCIATION WITH GOD

"Beloved, now we are the children of God." What is the reality of it? God clearly explains: *"if children,*

then heirs; heirs of God and joint heirs with Christ" (Rom. 8:17). But look at the tremendous, gigantic power of God behind our inheritance. First, we are adopted; then we receive an inheritance; then we are made coheirs with Jesus. There you come into it. Will you shiver like someone hesitating on the edge of a pool? Or will you take a plunge into omnipotence and find the waters are not as cold as people told you? Dare you let the warmth of the power of God make you see your inheritance in the Spirit? No, you will see something better than that. God touches our souls, making our whole bodies cry out for the living God. Glory!

Do you want God? Do you want fellowship in the Spirit? Do you want to walk with Him? Do you desire communion with Him? Everything else is no good. You want the association with God, and God says, *"I will come in to* [you] *and dine with* [you], *and* [you] *with Me"* (Rev. 3:20). Hallelujah! We can attain spiritual maturity, fullness of Christ, a place where God becomes the perfect Father and the Holy Spirit has a rightful place now as never before.

The Holy Spirit breathes through us, enabling us to say, "You are my Father; You are my Father." Because you have been adopted, *"God has sent forth the Spirit of His Son into your hearts, crying out, 'Abba, Father!'"* (Gal. 4:6). Oh, it is wonderful. May God the Holy Spirit grant to us that richness of His pleasure, that unfolding of His will, that consciousness of His smile upon us. There is *"no condemnation"* (Rom. 8:1). We find that *"the law of the Spirit of life"* makes us *"free from the law of sin and death"* (v. 2). Glory!

Sonship

The Spirit is having His perfect way because if we see the truth as clearly as God intends for us to see it, we will all be made so much richer, looking forward to the Blessed One who is coming again. Here we are, face to face with the facts. God has shown us different aspects of the Spirit. He has shown us the pavilion of splendor. He has revealed to us the power of the relationship of sonship. He has shown us that those who are God's children bear His image. They actively claim the rights of their adoption. They speak, and it is done. They bind the things that are loose, and loose the things that are bound (Matt. 16:19). And the perfection of sonship is so evident that more and more people are becoming children of God. They joyfully sing:

> I know the Lord, I know the Lord,
> I know the Lord's laid His hands on me.
> Oh, I know the Lord, I know the Lord,
> I know the Lord's laid His hands on me.

Do you believe it? Let us see you act it. Beloved, God the Holy Spirit has a perfect plan to make us a movement. There is a difference between a movement and a monument. A movement is something that is always active. A monument is something that is erected on a corner and neither speaks nor moves, but there is a tremendous lot of humbug and nonsense to get it in place. It is silent and does nothing. A movement is where God comes into the very being of a person, making him active for God. He is God's property, God's mouthpiece, God's eyes, and God's hands. God will *"sanctify you completely"* (1 Thess. 5:23).

The sanctification of the eyes, the hands, the mouth, the ears—to be so controlled by the Spirit who lives within us—is a wonderful place for God to bring us to. *"Beloved, now we are children of God; and it has not yet been revealed what we shall be"* (1 John 3:1–2). What a great thought: to be heirs, *"joint heirs with Christ"* (Rom. 8:17); to receive revelations and kindnesses from God; to have God dwell within man. The believer is filled, moved, and intensified until he takes wing. It would not take a trumpet to rouse him, for he is already on the wing, and he will land very soon. He would hear God's voice no matter how much noise surrounded him.

We read in 1 Corinthians 2:9: *"But as it is written: 'Eye has not seen, nor ear heard, nor have entered into the heart of man the things which God has prepared for those who love Him.'"*

Everything that is going to help you, you have to make yours. *"God has prepared."* He has stored it up already. You don't need a stepladder to get to it. It is ready to be handed out to you when you become joined with Him. When you walk with Him, He will either drop everything He has on you or take you where you are to remain forever.

Beloved, it is impossible in our finite condition to estimate the lovingkindness or the measureless mind of God. When we come into like-mindedness with the Word, instead of looking at the Word, we begin to see what God has for us in the Word. This is a very inexhaustible subject, but I pray that God will make us an inexhaustible people. I want you to be able to say:

> Me with a quenchless thirst inspire,
> A longing, infinite desire

Fill my craving heart.
  Less than Thyself You do not give,
Thy might within me now to live.
  Come, all Thou hast.

God, please come and make it impossible for me to ever be satisfied but to always have a quenchless thirst for You, the living God. Then I will not be overtaken. Then I will be ready. Then I will have shining eyes, filled with delight as they look at the Master.

THE SON OF GOD REVEALED

You ask, "Can we see the Master?" Here, look at Him. His Word is Spirit and life-giving. This is the breath, the Word of Jesus. Through the Holy Spirit, men have written and spoken. Here is the life. Here is the witness. Here is the truth. Here is the Son of God *"revealed from faith to faith"* (Rom. 1:17), from heart to heart, from vision to vision, until we all come into perfect unity of fellowship into the fullness of Christ.

There it is, beloved. Look! *"Now we are children of God."* If you are there, we can take a step further. But if you are not there, you may hear but not cross over. There is something about the Word of God that benefits the hearer who has faith, but if the hearer does not have faith, it will not profit.

The future is what you are today, not what you are going to be tomorrow. This is the day when God makes the future possible. When God reveals something to you today, tomorrow is filled with a further illumination of God's possibility for you.

Do you dare to come into the place of omnipotence, of wonderment? Do you dare to say to God, "I am ready for all that You have for me"? It will mean living a pure and holy life. It will mean living a sanctified, a separate life. It will mean your heart is so perfect and your prospects are so divinely separated that you say to the world, "Goodbye."

An Interpretation of Tongues:

Holiness is the habitation of Your house. Purity, righteousness, and truth are God's glorified position in the Spirit. The great desire of the Master is to make sons of God, for many sons He will gather into glory.

Listen to what God has to say. Everything must be absolutely the Word, so I only speak to you by the Word. Let us read Hebrews 2:6–10:

But one testified in a certain place, saying: "What is man that You are mindful of him, or the son of man that You take care of him? You have made him a little lower than the angels; You have crowned him with glory and honor, and set him over the works of Your hands. You have put all things in subjection under his feet." For in that He put all in subjection under him, He left nothing that is not put under him. But now we do not yet see all things put under him. But we see Jesus, who was made a little lower than the angels, for the suffering of death crowned with glory and honor, that He, by the grace of God, might taste death for everyone. For it was fitting for Him, for whom are

*all things and by whom are all things, in
bringing many sons to glory, to make the captain of their salvation perfect through sufferings.* (Heb. 2:6–10)

This second chapter of Hebrews describes the
mighty, glorified position for the children of God.
God wants me to announce it to every heart, like a
great trumpet call. The plan is to bring you to glory
as a child clothed with the power of the gifts, graces,
ministries, and operations. You are to be clothed
with the majesty of heaven. This is like heaven to
me. My very body is filled with thoughts of heaven.

Seeing that these things are so, what manner of
persons should we be? We should be keeping our
eyes upon Him that we may be ready for the Rapture. Oh, brothers and sisters, what immense pleasure God has for us! There is no limit to the sober-
mindedness God is bringing us to so that we may be
able to understand all that God has planned for us.
Oh, that we may look not on the things that are, but
with eyes of purity see only the invisible Son. Having
our whole bodies illuminated by the power of the
Holy Spirit, we grow in grace, in faith, and in Christ-
likeness until there is no difference between us and
Him.

Let me give you the Word if you can receive it:
"As He is, so are we in this world" (1 John 4:17).
What a word! Who dares to believe it? Only God can
take us to such heights, depths, lengths, and
breadths in the Spirit. Are you prepared to go all the
way? Are you willing for your heart to have only one
attraction? Are you willing to have only one Love?

Are you willing for Him to become your perfect Bridegroom?

The more bridelike we are, the more we love to hear the Bridegroom's voice; the less bridelike we are, the less we long for His Word. If you cannot rest without it, if it becomes your food day and night, if you eat and drink of it, His life will be in you, and when He appears, you will go with Him. Help us, Jesus!

How many are prepared to reveal yourself before the King? Are you prepared to yield to His call, yield to His will, yield to His desires? The Word has been preached; the Spirit has been speaking to you. How many are going to say, "At all costs I will go through!" Who says so? Who means it? Are you determined? Is your soul on the wing? Make a full consecration to God right now. It is between you and God. You are going now to enter the presence of God. Come clean with everything in the presence of God!

18

That I May Know Him

et us pray for God to enlarge our vision. I believe that He will. By His power, He will bring us into like-minded precious faith to believe all that the Scriptures say. The Scriptures are so deep that one can never enter into their truths without being enlarged by God. Beloved, one thing is certain: God can do it. *"All things that pertain to life and godliness"* (2 Pet. 1:3) are contained in the pursuit. We seek a faith that will not have a dim sight but will clear everything and claim all that God puts before it. And so I pray that God will reveal the depths of His righteousness that we may no longer be poor but very rich in God by His Spirit. Beloved, it is God's thought to make us all very rich *"in the grace and knowledge of our Lord and Savior Jesus Christ"* (2 Pet. 3:18).

RIGHTEOUSNESS IS FROM GOD

We have before us a message that is full of height, depth, length, and width, a message that came out of brokenness of spirit and the loss and enduring of all things. It is a message where flesh and all that relates to this world had to come to nothing. God can take us into this spiritual plane with Himself where we may be grounded in all knowledge. We can become so established in spiritual matters that we will always be lifted by God. Men try to lift themselves, but there is no inspiration in that. But when you are lifted by the Spirit, things come into perfect harmony, and you go forth right on to victory. That is a grand place to come to where we *"rejoice in Christ Jesus, and have no confidence in the flesh"* (Phil. 3:3). Paul adds, *"Though I also might have confidence in the flesh"* (v. 4). Although Paul had kept the law blamelessly, it was not his own performance in which he had confidence.

Oh, that is the greatest of all, when the Lord Jesus has the reins. Then we no longer have anything to boast about because all our righteousness that is determined by how perfectly we keep the law ceases. It is beautiful as we gaze upon the perfect Jesus. Jesus so exceeds everything else. For this reason, Paul felt that whatever he was, whatever he had been, whatever he had accomplished, he considered *"rubbish"* (v. 8). He could not achieve righteousness in his own strength.

BROKENNESS PRECEDES BLESSING

We must acknowledge our helplessness and nothingness. Although laboring in the Spirit is painful, God can lift the burden from us. I have had those days when I feel burdened. I have had it this morning, but now God is lifting the heaviness. And I say, brother and sister, unless God brings us into a place of brokenness of spirit, unless God remolds us in the great plan of His will for us, the best of us will utterly fail. But when we are absolutely taken in hand by the almighty God, God turns even our weakness into strength. He makes even that barren, helpless, groaning cry come forth, so that men and women are reborn in the travail. There is a place where our helplessness is touched by the power of God and where we come out shining as *"gold refined in the fire"* (Rev. 3:18).

There is no hope for Pentecost unless we come to God in our brokenness. It was on the cross that our Lord died with a broken heart. Pentecost came out of jeering and sneering. It included being mocked and beaten and an offer of sour wine. He received an unfair judgment and a cross that He had to bear. But, glory to God, Pentecost rings out this morning for you through the words, *"It is finished!"* (John 19:30). And now because it is finished, we can take the same place that He took and rise out of that death in majestic glory with the resurrection touch of heaven. People will know that God has done something for us.

BE MADE NEW

Daily, there must be a revival touch in our hearts. He must change us after His fashion. We are to be made new all the time. There is no such thing as having all grace and knowledge. God wants us to begin with these words of power found in Philippians 3 and never stop, but go on to perfection. God wants us to reach the blessings in these verses today:

> *But what things were gain to me, these I have counted loss for Christ. Yet indeed I also count*

> *all things loss for the excellence of the knowl-*
> *edge of Christ Jesus my Lord, for whom I have*
> *suffered the loss of all things, and count them*
> *as rubbish, that I may gain Christ.*
>
> (Phil. 3:7–8)

Turn to Hebrews 10:32: *"But recall the former days in which, after you were illuminated, you endured a great struggle with sufferings."* I am positive that no man can attain like-mindedness except by the illumination of the Spirit.

God has been speaking to me over and over that I must urge people to receive the baptism of the Holy Spirit. In the baptism of the Holy Spirit, there is unlimited grace and endurance as the Spirit reveals Himself to us. The excellency of Christ can never be understood apart from illumination. And I find that the Holy Spirit is the great Illuminator who makes me understand all the depths of Him. I must witness about Christ. Jesus said to Thomas, *"Thomas, because you have seen Me, you have believed. Blessed are those who have not seen and yet have believed"* (John 20:29).

There is a revelation that brings us into touch with Him where we get all and see right into the fullness of Christ. As Paul saw the depths and heights of the grandeur, he longed that he might win Him. Before his conversion, in his passion and zeal, Paul would do anything to bring Christians to death. His passion raged like a mighty lion. As he was going to Damascus, he heard the voice of Jesus saying, *"Saul, Saul, why are you persecuting Me?"* (Acts 9:4). What touched him was the tenderness of God.

That I May Know Him

Friends, it is always God's tenderness that reaches us. He comes to us in spite of our weakness and depravity. If somebody came to oppose us, we would stand our ground, but when He comes to forgive us, we do not know what to do. Oh, to win Christ! A thousand things in the nucleus of a human heart need softening a thousand times a day. There are things in us that unless God shows us *"the excellence of the knowledge of Christ Jesus"* (Phil. 3:8), we will never be broken and brought to ashes. But God will do it. We will not merely be saved, but we will be saved a thousand times over! Oh, this transforming regeneration by the power of the Spirit of the living God makes me see there is a place to *"gain Christ"* (v. 8), that I may stand complete there. As He was, so am I to be. The Scriptures declare that we can be:

> *Found in Him, not having* [our] *own righteousness, which is from the law, but that which is through faith in Christ, the righteousness which is from God by faith.* (v. 9)

We cannot depend upon our works, but upon the faithfulness of God, being able under all circumstances to be hidden in Him, covered by the almighty presence of God. The Scriptures tell us that we are in Christ and Christ is in God. What is able to move you from this place of omnipotent power? *"Shall tribulation, or distress, or persecution, or famine, or nakedness, or peril, or sword?"* (Rom. 8:35). Oh, no! Will life, or death, or principalities, or powers? (v. 38). No, *"we are more than conquerors through Him who loved us"* (v. 37).

FOUND IN HIM

I must be *"found in Him"* (Phil. 3:9). There is a place of seclusion, a place of rest and faith in Jesus where there is nothing else like it. Jesus came to His disciples on the water, and they were terrified. But He said, *"It is I; do not be afraid"* (Matt. 14:27). My friend, He is always there. He is there in the storm as well as in the peace; He is there in adversity. When will we know He is there? When we are *"found in Him,"* not having our own work, our own plan, but resting in the omnipotent plan of God. Oh, is it possible for the child of God to fail? It is not possible, for *"He who keeps Israel shall neither slumber nor sleep"* (Ps. 121:4). He will watch over us continually, but we must be *"found in Him."*

I know there is a secret place in Jesus that is open to us today. My brother, my sister, you have been nearly weighed down with troubles. They have almost crushed you. Sometimes you thought you would never get out of this place of difficulty, but you have no idea that behind the whole thing, God has been working a plan greater than all.

Today is a resurrection day. We must know the resurrection of His power in brokenness of spirit: *"That I may know Him and the power of His resurrection"* (Phil. 3:10). Jesus said to Martha, *"I am the resurrection and the life"* (John 11:25). Oh, to know the resurrection power, to know the rest of faith. Any one of us, without exception, can reach this happiness in the Spirit. There is something different between saying you have faith and then being pressed into a tight corner and proving that you have faith. If you dare to believe, it will be done according to your faith: *"Whatever things you ask when you pray, believe that you receive them, and you will have them"* (Mark 11:24). Jesus is *"the resurrection and the life"* (John 11:25). With God's help, we must gain this life. We can reach it with the knowledge that He will make us as white as snow, as pure and holy as He, that we may go with boldness to His *"throne of grace"* (Heb. 4:16). Boldness is in His holiness. Boldness is in His righteousness. Boldness is in His truth. You cannot have the boldness of faith if you are not pure. What blessed words follow: *"the fellowship of His sufferings"* (Phil. 3:10). Remember, unless that fellowship touches us, we will never have much power.

When the Spirit of the Lord moves within you, you will be broken down and then built up. Jesus came forth in the glory of the Father, filled with all the fullness of God. It was God's plan before *"the foundation of the world"* (Matt. 25:34). God loved the fearful, helpless human race, with all its blackness and hideousness of sin, and He provided the way for redemption. May God give us such *"fellowship of His sufferings"* (Phil. 3:10) that when we see a person afflicted with cancer, we will pray right through until the disease is struck dead. When we see a bent and helpless woman or a man who is weak and sick, may God give us compassion and a fellowship with them that will lighten their heavy burdens and set them free. How often we have missed the victory because we did not have the Lord's compassion at the needed moment. We failed to pray with a broken heart.

Is there anything more? Oh, yes, we must see the next thing. We must be *"conformed to His death"* (Phil. 3:10). *"Unless a grain of wheat falls into the ground and dies, it remains alone; but if it dies, it produces much grain"* (John 12:24). God wants you to see that unless you are dead indeed, unless you come to a perfect crucifixion, unless you die with Him, you are not in the *"fellowship of His sufferings"* (Phil. 3:10). May God move upon us in this life to bring us into an absolute death, not merely to talk about it. In this way, Christ's life may be made manifest. With Paul, we can say:

> *I do not count myself to have apprehended; but one thing I do, forgetting those things which are behind and reaching forward to those things which are ahead, I press toward the goal for the prize of the upward call of God in Christ Jesus.* (vv. 13–14)

The Lord wants us to understand that we must come to a place where our natural life ceases, and by the power of God, we rise into a life where God rules and reigns. Do you long to know Him? Do you long to be *"found in Him"* (v. 9)? Your longing will be satisfied today. I ask you to fall in the presence of God. All you who want to know God, yield to His mighty power, and obey the Spirit.

19

Our Inheritance

His divine power has given to us all things that pertain to life and godliness, through the knowledge of Him who called us by glory and virtue.
—2 Peter 1:3

Many people make wills and appoint someone to carry out their final requests. After the person dies, very often those people who have had property left to them never get it because of unfaithful stewards who have been left in charge. But there is one will that has been left, and He who made the whole will is our Lord Jesus Christ. After dying, He rose to carry out His own will. And now we may have all that has been left to us by Him: all the inheritance, all the blessings, all the power, all the life, and all the victory. All His promises are ours because He is risen. I believe the Lord wants us to know our inheritance.

Because He is risen as a faithful High Priest, He is here to help us understand His divine principles. May God provide us with a clear knowledge of what He means for us in these days. He has called us to great banquets and wants us to bring good appetites to His table.

It is a serious thing to come to a banquet of the Lord and not be able to eat anything. We must have very thirsty conditions and hungry souls. Then we can have what is prepared for us. We can be *"strengthened with might through His Spirit in the inner man"* (Eph. 3:16). May the Lord take us into His treasures now.

A DIVINE MIND

We will find out that the truth is always revealed to us through Christ. All the fullness is in Him. All the glories surround Him. All the divine virtue flows from Him. We must understand that God is bringing us into the place where we can understand what He means by *"things that pertain to life and godliness, through the knowledge of Him."* God has brought us from one step to another. First, He gave us a glimpse of faith. Then, He gave us assurance of the faith on the principles of the groundwork of Christ being the foundation of all things. Now, the Lord wants to show us how this virtue can remain in us. We must reach to attain this virtue.

What is virtue? Oh, friends, Paul received these divine powers, which he calls *"the effective working of His power"* (Eph. 3:7). He is talking about the divine infilling, which has to fill the whole body with life, virtue, grace, power, and faith. There are no limitations. God is the Executive of the kingdom of heaven. He has power in our body as we open ourselves to Him. We recognize His immeasurable fullness as He reveals Himself to us.

Our Inheritance

So, beloved, God wants us to understand that whatever it costs, whatever it means, we must have a personal incoming of this life of God, this Holy Spirit, this divine person.

I want you to think about what it really means to receive the Holy Spirit. We are born again *"not of corruptible seed but incorruptible, through the word of God"* (1 Pet. 1:23). The Word *"lives and abides forever"* (v. 23). We are born again by the incorruptible power of God. It is His plan for us. This divine power is beyond anything that the human mind can conceive. We must have a divine mind in order to understand divine things.

Our lives must be changed by His grace. Our bodies must become a *"temple of the Holy Spirit"* (1 Cor. 6:19). We must *"have the mind of Christ"* (1 Cor. 2:16). And we must understand that God has come to change us into His image, filling us with His power.

Jesus came into this world, but He had an eternal perspective. Jesus lived in the present but often spoke of the future. Beloved, there is a future, but we must not neglect the present. Whatever God has designed for man, we must claim it now. We will always have greater demonstrations of power if we are living in the now instead of in the future. We must experience a now power, a now blessing, a now God, a now heaven, a now glory, a now virtue.

An Interpretation of Tongues:

It is the Spirit that works in us all these divine plans so that He may build us on the foundations of the living Word, which lives, which always quickens and moves. Builds

high, higher, higher, into and with love. It is
always in a higher sense because God has no
lower means.

He wants us to go higher and higher. Oh, for a
heavenly sight and a divine touch of God today. One
touch of deity, one flash of light, one moment in His
presence, one touch of the infinite Trinity makes us
strong; in a moment, we are able to see all things as
He sees them.

An Interpretation of Tongues:
Oh, I must never cease until I reach that
which God has for me, for I must be for others
what He wants me to be.

It is a divine virtue to recognize the presence of
the Holy Spirit. May it be said of us as it was said of
Stephen: *"A man full of faith and the Holy Spirit"*
(Acts 6:5). Barnabas was also a good man filled with
the Holy Spirit and faith. (See Acts 15:25–26.) There
is a divine place of purity where the unclean can
never put their feet. It is a holy place where the pure
in heart can see God (Matt. 5:8). Only through following God's directions can you get to that place.
God's way is called the *"Highway of Holiness"* (Isa.
35:8), and He longs to bring us into that place where
we can hear the voice of God, see the form of God,
understand the ways of God, and walk in communion with God. In this place, divine virtue flows.

Once at a very late meeting being held outdoors,
I was surrounded by a great number of people. God
was saving people, and oh, the joy I felt in pointing
people to Jesus. When I went home, my family said

to me, "Aunt Mary is going home, and Uncle Sam would like you to see her before she bids farewell." I went there, not knowing what to say but "Goodbye." As I came close to her bed, I was impressed to stretch out my hand. What there is in a hand! What there is in a person touched by the power of God, no one can tell. As my hand touched her hand, the divine virtue of heaven flowed through her dying body and brought her into perfect life, perfect as she ever was, instantaneously brought back from death into life, joy, and peace.

There is a virtue; there is a truth. God must manifest His power until everything we touch moves at the power of God. Paul knew it, the apostles had a clear understanding of it, and Jesus spoke about it. When the woman who touched the hem of Christ's garment was healed, she felt His power. Knowing immediately that *"power had gone out of Him,"* Jesus asked, *"Who touched My clothes?"* (Mark 5:30).

There is a power that goes through the human body to another body. I see that it is in perfect alignment with the Scriptures that we *"lay hands on the sick, and they will recover"* (Mark 16:18).

There is a truth in John's gospel that some have never understood. May God reveal it to us now:

> *Most assuredly, I say to you, We speak what We know and testify what We have seen, and you do not receive Our witness. If I have told you earthly things and you do not believe, how will you believe if I tell you heavenly things? No one has ascended to heaven but He who came down from heaven, that is, the Son of Man who is in heaven.* (John 3:11–13)

A DIVINE SOURCE

Now, look at that electric light. It is illuminating the place because of the generator. It has a receiver and a transmitter. Although the wires are important, it is the power of the generator that is sending forth the light through those wires. Likewise, every man who is born of God is receiving life from God. God is the source of power. Inside man's heart and mind is the wire that receives the revelation and transmits the illumination. In order to keep it functioning perfectly, it must always return to the source of power. And so it is with everyone who is born of God. He is kept alive by a power that he cannot see but he can feel, a power that is generated in glory, comes down into earthen vessels, and returns to the throne of God.

We are receiving and transmitting all the time. When we stop for a moment to place our hands upon a needy case, the supernatural goes through that person and brings life. God wants us to know that He is the source of divine glory, divine virtue, and perfect knowledge.

The Holy Spirit is the great Motivator of us all. He receives all, He disburses all, and He sends out the wonderful manifestations after He has had the call. So we must have life in the Spirit, united, illuminated, transformed all the time by this glorious regenerating power of the Spirit. May God reveal that it is for us all. Such a manifestation of the life and power of God will be given to us until there will be neither barrenness nor unfruitfulness, but rather a surrender to all His will. Hallelujah!

Our Inheritance

An Interpretation of Tongues:
It is that which God has designed from the beginning. It is no new thing. It is as old as God. It lasts as long as eternity. We are, we will be, forever with Him. He has created us for this purpose: that we should be the sons of God with power, with promise, with life, for all the world.

Oh, brothers and sisters, don't tell me that we have received all the fullness of the Spirit, an immeasurable portion! Don't tell me that there are any limitations to it. It comes in floods that we cannot contain. We drink and drink and drink again, and yet, we are still dry. Saints of God, the more of this joy you get, the more you require, the more you desire. It is God in you who longs for all His fullness to come into you, praise His name. But we must be partakers of it.

A DIVINE GLORY

Two words here are closely connected. They are beautiful words, full of meaning for this moment. Let me read them: *"Through the knowledge of Him who called us by glory and virtue."*

A lot of people have a great misunderstanding about glory. Glory is always an expression. For instance, on the Day of Pentecost, it was necessary that the moving by the mighty rushing wind should be made evident in the upper room. It was also important that the disciples should be clothed with *"tongues, as of fire"* (Acts 2:3). Then it was significant that the whole group gathered there should receive not only the fire but also the rushing wind, the personality of the Spirit in the wind. The divine order is in the wind, and all the manifestation of the glory is in the wind.

Now let me express it. The inward man instantly receives the Holy Spirit with great joy and blessedness. He cannot express it. It is beyond his expression. He received the power of the Spirit, which is the Word. I want you to notice that when the Holy Spirit is in the body, this divine power, this personality, this breath of God, takes the things of Jesus and utters them by this expressive wind. Like a river, He sends forth the utterances of the Spirit.

Then again, when the body is filled with joy, sometimes it is so inexpressible. Thrown on the canvas of the mind, the mind moves the tongue to speak power, love, and joy to us from the very depths of the heart. By the same process, the Spirit, which is the breath of God, brings forth the manifestation of the glory.

When God speaks, there is always glory. Peter writes about being on the holy mountain:

> *For we did not follow cunningly devised fables when we made known to you the power and coming of our Lord Jesus Christ, but were eyewitnesses of His majesty. For He received from God the Father honor and glory when such a voice came to Him from the Excellent Glory: "This is My beloved Son, in whom I am well pleased."* (2 Pet. 1:16–17)

Sometimes people wonder how and why it is that the Holy Spirit is always expressing Himself in words. It cannot be otherwise. You couldn't understand it otherwise. You cannot understand God by shakings, and yet shakings may be in perfect order sometimes. There isn't any manifestation of the body—shakings, rollings, jumpings, and all kinds of things that are allowed—that is a manifestation of God. Only the utterances are manifestations of God. The others may be so mixed with the flesh and the Spirit that it would take a great deal of divine intuition and divine revelation to discriminate between the Spirit and flesh.

But you can always tell when the Spirit moves and brings forth utterances. These utterances, not waving of hands and shakings of body, magnify God. But the Holy Spirit has a perfect plan. He comes right through every man who is so filled and brings divine utterances that we may understand what the mind of the Lord is.

You notice I give all my addresses by inspiration. I dare not work things out in my mind before I come. If I did, I would get out of the plan of God. I have to come to you with the bare Word of God and expect the Holy Spirit to enlighten it. I must read into my heart the perfect law of liberty. If I came to you with a fixed arrangement of an address, the whole thing would come from my humanity. But I cannot afford to be natural. I can only afford to be supernatural now. I cannot afford to be anything less than directed entirely by the Holy Spirit. If I turn to any other plan, then I lose the unction, the power, the revelation of what God has. When I come into the presence of God, He takes the things of the Spirit and reveals them to me. Our hearts are comforted and built up. And there is no way to warm a heart more than by the heart that first touched the flame. There must be the heavenly fires burning within.

We are born of the Spirit, and nothing but the Spirit of God can feed that spiritual life. We must live in it, feed in it, walk in it, talk in it, and sleep in it. Hallelujah! We must always be in the Holy Spirit whether asleep or awake. There is a place for man in the Holy Spirit where God has him; he is lost to every man, but he is never lost to God. God can find him any time He wants him. Oh, hallelujah!

I want to turn to three Scriptures so that we may see what they say about glory and not be deceived. *"Therefore my heart is glad, and my glory rejoices; My flesh also will rest in hope"* (Ps. 16:9). The psalmist's rejoicing brings forth the glory. It was because his heart was glad. In Psalm 108, we see another side of glory: *"O God, my heart is steadfast; I will sing and give praise, even with my glory"* (v. 1). So you see, glory is a manifestation of language. It is when the body is filled with the powers of God. Then the tongue is the only thing that can express the glory. And God has given us tongues so that we can express the glory, the glory of God.

Glory is not a halo. It is a presence, and the presence always comes by the tongue bringing forth the revelations of God. In Acts, we see yet another aspect to glory:

> *For David says concerning Him: "I foresaw the LORD always before my face, for He is at my right hand, that I may not be shaken. Therefore my heart rejoiced, and my tongue was glad; moreover my flesh also will rest in hope."* (Acts 2:25–26)

Our Inheritance

You will always find that God works this way. First, He fills us with His power. Then He gives us verbal expressions by the same Spirit moving within us in order that the manifestation of the Spirit will be evident outwardly as well. Therefore, *"out of the abundance of the heart the mouth speaks"* (Matt. 12:34).

What is all this about? I want you to notice that virtue and glory will be inexpressible conditions sometimes. You will find out that virtue has to be transmitted, and you will find out that glory has to be expressed. And so God, by filling us with the Holy Spirit, has brought into us that which He has in the glory so that out of us may come forth His glory.

The world's needs, our manifestations, revivals, and all conditions are first settled in heaven, then worked out on earth. So we must be in touch with God Almighty to bring out on the face of the earth all the things that God has in the heavens. This is an ideal for us. May God help us not to forsake the sense of holy communion we enjoy privately so that we may manifest His glory publicly.

We must see the face of the Lord and understand His workings. There are things that God says to me that I know must take place. It doesn't matter what people say. I have been face to face with some of the most trying moments of men's lives when it meant so much to me to keep the vision and hold fast to what God had said.

A man must be in an immovable condition. The voice of God must mean to him more than what he sees, feels, or hears. He must have an originality born in heaven, transmitted by tongues, or expressed in some way. We must bring heaven to earth. That is our godly purpose.

A DIVINE NATURE

We must enter into this because we have to be partakers of His divine nature. The priceless promises that we have been given enable us to *"be partakers of the divine nature, having escaped the corruption that is in the world through lust"* (2 Pet. 1:4). Turn to Romans 8:2: *"For the law of the Spirit of life in Christ Jesus has made me free from the law of sin and death."* God wants us to see that there are two laws, but the *"law of the Spirit of life in Christ Jesus"* is different from the *"law of sin and death."* One looks on the divine principles, which make me know that I am free.

Let me turn to that law of the Spirit. This same life that is the *"law of the Spirit of life"* brings us into the same attitude of being partakers of His divine nature. You see, it is a divine life. I have two lives. I have a spiritual life and a natural life.

I hope no one will ever be so foolish as to believe that the natural life is done away with. You will always have it as long as you live. It may be there for great advantages. For instance, I thank God for my natural life this morning, which has enabled me to walk and to dress myself. I thank God for the natural life that has brought us here. It is the natural body that brought your spiritual perception into a holy meeting, and your natural body is necessary to bring you to a place where you can feed your spiritual desires.

But we must understand that the natural has only a certain part to play. It is always to advance the control the Spirit of the living God has over our bodies. The spiritual life is so powerful. It can bring to death the natural man, until the righteousness of God can so permeate the whole body that the virtues of Christ are as much in the fingers as in the hand. It is the divine life, the divine virtue of our Lord Jesus Christ.

Then while we walk about, it is absolutely true that we have no desire for the world because our desires are greater than the world. You cannot fascinate a man of God with gold, houses, or lands. We seek a country, a *"house not made with hands, eternal in the heavens"* (2 Cor. 5:1). And if this mortal body will be put off, the heavenly body will be put on. And we are waiting and longing with an expression, with an inward joy, with a great leap of life, waiting to jump into that.

An Interpretation of Tongues:
He has designed the plan. He has the unfolding of the purpose. He is the grandeur of the principles. He lays the foundation of the spiritual life, quickened always by His own life, for He is our life, and when He will appear, we will be like Him. He will appear!

Beloved, there is a longing in the soul. There is a travail in the spirit, a yielding of the will, the blending of the life that only gives utterances as He wishes. I believe God is bringing us to a longing for these utterances in the Spirit.

Oh, this is a lovely verse. See, there is so much depth in it, but it is all real from heaven. It is as divinely appointed for this meeting as when the Holy Spirit was upon Peter, and He brings it out for us. I will read it again, for it is life, breath, and marrow.

It moves me. I must live in this grace: *"As His divine power has given to us all things that pertain to life and godliness, through the knowledge of Him who called us by glory and virtue."*

You cannot get away from Him. He is the center of all things. He moves the earth, transforms beings, can live in every mind, and plans every thought. Oh, He is there all the time.

The Holy Spirit has only language. There is no language on earth that man has formed; it takes the Holy Spirit to form a language. You will find if you go to one of the epistles, when Paul has finished, he is full of the strength of the Spirit. The Spirit breathes through him, yet he comes to a place where he feels he must stop. There are greater things than even he can utter. Prayer, the breath of the Almighty, breathes through the human soul. There He breathes through Paul.

In Ephesians 3:20, you find words that no human could ever think or plan. They are so mighty, so of God: *"Now to Him who is able to do exceedingly abundantly above all that we ask or think, according to the power that works in us."* The mighty God of revelation through a man! There the Holy Spirit gave these words of grandeur to stir our hearts, to move our affections, to transform us altogether. This is ideal. This is God. Will we teach these words? Will we have them? Oh, they are ours. Will they remain ours? God has never put anything over on a pole you could not reach. God has brought His plan down to man.

Sometimes we have as much as we can digest, yet there are divine nuggets of precious truth held before our hearts. It makes you understand that there are yet heights, depths, lengths, and breadths of the knowledge of God that God has laid up for us (v. 18). We might truly say:

> My heavenly bank, my heavenly bank,
>   The house of God's treasure and store.
> I have plenty in here; I'm a real millionaire.

Glory is all in here. We are never to be poverty stricken anymore. We have an inward knowledge of an unfolding of a greater bank than ever the Rothschilds or any other child ever knew about. There it is stored up, nugget upon nugget, weights of glory, expression of the countenance of the invisible Christ to be seen.

God is shaking the earth and the foundations of all nationalities. Constantly, He is helping us to understand the principle in the Scriptures that can bring man freedom from the natural order of every institution. He wants to bring man to a place of holiness, righteousness, and God's peace, which passes all human understanding (Phil. 4:7). We must touch it. We must reach it. Praise God!

One thing is certain. God has brought us in on purpose to take us on. You say, "How will I be able to get all these things that are laid up for me?" Brothers and sisters, I know of no other way but through a *"broken and a contrite heart,"* which *"God...will not despise"* (Ps. 51:17).

A man asked me last night, "Don't you think I am baptized with the Holy Spirit?"

I said, "I don't know anything about you."

"I am willing for anything," he told me.

Then I knew he was not baptized. I never saw a man "willing for anything" that got anything. The man that gets anything is the man who goes after one thing. *"One thing have I desired of the LORD, that will I seek"* (Ps. 27:4). Whatever you want, make it one thing and get it.

What do you want? Make it one thing. You know better than I do what you want, and God knows what you want. That one thing you require is for you today. May God help you to move from your seats where you are and get that one thing. Determine to know the powers of the world to come, and you will see, for truly when Daniel set his mind to get all the things which were provided, God gave an abundance of other things which have not yet been fulfilled. So I remind you of one thing:

> *Ask, and it will be given to you; seek, and you will find; knock, and it will be opened to you. For everyone who asks receives, and he who seeks finds, and to him who knocks it will be opened.* (Matt. 7:7–8)

May God help you to take your own course, to do as the Spirit leads, and to leave everything in God's hands.

20

A Living Sacrifice

I beseech you therefore, brethren, by the mercies of
God, that you present your bodies a living sacrifice,
holy, acceptable to God, which is your reasonable
service. And do not be conformed to this world,
but be transformed by the renewing of your mind,
that you may prove what is that good
and acceptable and perfect will of God.
—Romans 12:1–2

ere we have the words of a man who had come right out of the ashes of broken faith, speaking to all the saints, saying: "He has brought me to the place where everything has gone on the altar. All that I have and all that I am is consecrated to God. Such a lovely place! Such a wealthy place! Such a rich place! And I want all the saints to come into the same place."

THE WEAKNESS OF THE FLESH

Flesh will interfere with us and stop our progress, but if the Spirit of the Lord is upon us, the flesh is brought to a place where we understand the truth of Romans 8:10: *"And if Christ is in you, the body is dead because of sin, but the Spirit is life because of righteousness."*

The moment flesh is dealt with and judgment comes to it, we are brought to a place of helplessness. The flesh has gone; it is dead, but the Spirit breathes life within us. The body is helpless, but it is dominated by the power of the Spirit until it longs to breathe and act in the Spirit. It is beautiful.

One of the greatest mercies that you will ever have will be a revelation to your heart of how to get rid of yourself. Boundless spiritual resources are available after the flesh no longer reigns. Bask in these words: *"Blessed are those who hunger and thirst for righteousness, for they shall be filled"* (Matt. 5:6). You cannot hunger and thirst after righteousness if you have any leanings toward the worldly life. The righteousness of God is a perfect development in your life of inward heart sanctification, where no defilement can enter, and the pure in heart always see God (v. 8). It is a deep death, and it is a great life. God makes it a holy sacrifice, and He accepts it as an offering. Then, when we have perfectly considered the whole thing, we come to the conclusion that it was a reasonable thing to do.

A Sensible Choice

Anything less than surrendering yourself completely to God is unreasonable because God has claimed us. In every way, we belong rightfully to Him. As you sit at the table where God in His great provision has amply supplied enough to satisfy your earthly needs, remember that a man is more capable of doing the mighty works of God and the will of God with a strong body than with a weak body. The strong body is never so richly in the presence of God as it is when it knows its weakness, for then there comes a real privilege. Strong bodies, strong minds, strong physiques, and strong muscles are wonderful, but they are no good until all is on the altar. Then God can flow through the body and give that person perfect life. He receives the resurrection life of the Spirit. Then his whole body is spiritual. It is severed from the natural, and he receives the fulfillment of the promise, *"Be strong in the Lord and in the power of His might"* (Eph. 6:10). The natural body is in perfect harmony with the Spirit to show forth the glory of God.

There is a Scripture that we seldom understand. This verse has taken me a long time to grasp: *"So then death is working in us, but life in you"* (2 Cor. 4:12). Only as death was manifested in the saints could life come to them. Death to us, life to you. That means absolutely nothing less than that everything you count on in life has to go, and as it goes, you are transformed. *"Death is working in us, but life in you."*

DYING TO LIVE

In the measure that you remain dead, you live forever: *"For the law of the Spirit of life in Christ Jesus has made* [you] *free from the law of sin and death"* (Rom. 8:2). You are *"transformed by the renewing of your mind."* The mind of Christ is in you, and your mind is subservient to the mind of Christ.

Submissively, Jesus offered His mind, body, and will. Wonderful Jesus. He lived as no one else ever has or will. He is beautiful. I am devoted to Him. I love the Word of God because Christ is in every verse, illuminating every chapter. The Word is the breath of God, and it is life to you. It is eternal life. May God enable us always to breathe it in.

21

Above All You Can Ask or Think

To Him who is able to do exceedingly abundantly above all that we ask or think...be glory.
—Ephesians 3:20–21

ead Ephesians 3 carefully. This is a lovely chapter on Paul's mission to the Gentiles whom God has grafted in. Paul writes that previously it had not been revealed *"that the Gentiles should be fellow heirs, of the same body, and partakers of* [God's] *promise in Christ"* (vv. 5–6). Paul had become a *"minister according to the gift of the grace of God given to* [him] *by the effective working of His power"* (v. 7). This power in Paul resulted in a very effective work. Although he was *"less than the least of all the saints"* (v. 8), he was given this grace of mystery and revelation. It came forth as a living reality of a living substance dwelling in him: *"to the intent that now the manifold wisdom of God might be made known by the church to the principalities and powers in the heavenly places"* (v. 10).

WISDOM

When we are completely humbled before God in a place where the Holy Spirit has full control, the wisdom of God is revealed to us. There alone, the vision comes to all His saints. We are now in the process of revelation. You must let the Holy Spirit perform His perfect function. I give myself to the leading of the manifold wisdom of God, *"in whom we have boldness and access with confidence through faith in Him"* (v. 12).

Boldness brings us into a place of access (Heb. 4:16), a place of confidence, laying hold, taking all off the table, and making it ours. In the human body, the Holy Spirit unfolds the mystery that we might know and have the revelation according to the will of God. The flesh is brought to a place of nonexistence, and the mighty power of God is shown to us. Paul responds by saying: *"I bow my knees to the Father"* (Eph. 3:14).

PRAYER

Jude speaks of praying in the Holy Spirit. There is no natural line of thought here, not one point in particular upon which the mind can rest, but what is predicted from the throne of glory. Then the tongue and all the divine attributes are displayed above all, exceedingly above all, so that the glory of God may be revealed in the face of Jesus. God cannot display the greater glory except through those coequal in the glory, *"for we are His workmanship, created in Christ Jesus for good works"* (Eph. 2:10). The Holy Spirit is the ideal and brings out the very essence of heaven through the human soul. We need the baptism of the Holy Spirit. Here we have the greatest liberty that can come to humanity; all the liberty of heaven is open to us. Praise the Father *"from whom the whole family in heaven and earth is named"* (Eph. 3:15).

I love the thought that the veil is so thin that the tie between the family of God in heaven and the family of God on earth is closer than ever. Christ is with them, and they are with us. What loftiness, reverence, and holiness! This wedlock and fellowship in the Spirit is a wonderful thing. It results in an infinite mind of fulfillment and glory. *"Are they not all ministering spirits?"* (Heb. 1:14). Who can help us more than those who have experienced the same trials as we? As the body is so fitly joined together by the effective working of His power, we are all one. Nothing separates us, but we look for the appearing of Jesus. He is there in glory, and they are with Him:

> *For the Lord Himself will descend from heaven with a shout, with the voice of an archangel, and with the trumpet of God. And the dead in Christ will rise first. Then we who are alive and remain shall be caught up together with them in the clouds to meet the Lord in the air. And thus we shall always be with the Lord.* (1 Thess. 4:16–17)

We can pray only as the Holy Spirit gives us the ability to express our thoughts. The Holy Spirit gives the highest principles through this prayer that the purposes of salvation are a continuous working and an increasing power all the time. The day that is coming will declare all things. We will be strengthened by the Spirit according to the riches of His glory.

GLORY

What is glory? All glory that ever comes is from Him. You have glory in the measure that you have the Son of glory in you. If you are filled with Jesus, you are filled with glory. When we have *"the spirit of wisdom and revelation in the knowledge of Him"* (Eph. 1:17), there is nothing to hinder the Holy Spirit from having control of our whole beings.

"That Christ may dwell in your hearts through faith" (Eph. 3:17). Faith is the production of all things. The Holy Spirit indwells and enlarges until the whole body is filled with Christ, and we are coming there in a very remarkable way. Did the Holy Spirit ever utter a prayer that no power could answer? In John 17:21, Jesus says: *"That they all may be one, as You, Father, are in Me, and I in You; that they also may be one in Us."* What works in us through being one with Him, through *"being rooted and grounded"* (Eph. 3:17)? Perfect love, which has justice wrapped up in it. The day is coming when the saints will say "Amen" to the judgments of God. Justice will do it. All the wood, hay, and stubble must be destroyed (1 Cor. 3:12), and we must be *"rooted and grounded"* in the Word.

I am a production of what God is forming, and I can arrest the gates of hell and laugh in the face of calamity and say, *"All things work together for good to those who love God"* (Rom. 8:28). *"Rooted and grounded in love"* (Eph. 3:17). Someone may leave me, but if I am grounded, it is for my good, and nothing can be against me but myself. We live for the glory of God. It is the Lord that establishes, strengthens, and upholds the weak, enabling them to withstand difficulties and to triumph in the day of battle. God is with you *"to do exceedingly abundantly above all that* [you] *ask or think."*

FAITH

Are we children of circumstances or children of faith? In our humanity, we may be troubled by the blowing of the wind. As it blows, it whispers fearfulness; but if you are *"rooted and grounded,"* you can stand the tests, and it is only then that you *"may be able to comprehend...what is the width and length and depth and height; to know the love of Christ which passes knowledge"* (Eph. 3:18–19). It is an addition sum to meet every missionary's needs, to display God's power, enlarging what needs to be quickened.

What does Paul mean by the width of Christ's love? It is recognizing that God is sufficient in every circumstance. The length of His love indicates that God is in everything. God is in the depths and the heights! God is always lifting you, and the truth in that verse is enough for anyone in any circumstance to triumph. He *"is able to do exceedingly abundantly above all that we can ask or think,"* not according to the mind of Paul, but *"according to the power that works in us"* (v. 20). Simplicity of heart can broaden one's perspective, but this fullness is an ideal power of God in the human soul, enlarging every part. God is there instead of you to make you full, and you are full as your faith reaches out to be filled with all the fullness of God.

The power of the Lord was present to heal. His fullness of power flowed out of the disciples to others. In Acts 1, we see the power of God revealed as Jesus was lifted up to where He was before—into the presence of God. Jesus Christ showed the power of God in human flesh. The fullness of the Godhead was bodily manifested in Jesus (Col. 2:9). John says that *"in Him was life, and the life was the light of men"* (John 1:4). His substance revealed the fullness of God. How can it be fulfilled in me, you ask? The Scripture provides the answer: He is *"able to do exceedingly abundantly above all that we can ask or think."* It is filled there in the glory. But it's a tremendous thing. God will have to do something. Beloved, it is not according to your mind at all but according to the mind of God, according to the revelation of the Spirit. *"Above all that we can ask or think."* The blood has been poured out.

THE HOLY SPIRIT HAS BEEN GIVEN TO US

Truly, we are not worthy, but He is worthy. He will do more than we can even ask. How can it be possible? God puts it in your heart. He can do it. We hear much about rates of interest, but if you will faithfully follow God, He will add, enlarge, and lift you all the time, adding compound interest. Five percent? No! A thousand percent, a million percent! If you are willing, if holiness is the purpose of your heart, it will be done, for God is in His place. Will you be in the plan *"according to the power that works in* [you]*"* (Eph. 3:20)? Whatever you are at any time, it will be by His effective power, lifting, controlling, and carrying you in constant rest and peace; it is *"according to the power that works in* [you]." Let all the people say: *"To Him be glory in the church by Christ Jesus to all generations, forever and ever. Amen"* (v. 21).

22

This Grace

When we are filled with the joy of the Lord, there comes forth a glad "Praise the Lord!" David experienced that joy and proclaimed: *"Let everything that has breath praise the LORD"* (Ps. 150:6). It is a tragedy if there is not a divine spring within you bubbling forth with praise. God wants you to be so filled with the Spirit that your whole life is a praise. How my soul longs for you to catch fire.

Four symbols divinely ascertained or revealed by the Lord are fire, love, zeal, and faith. Fire burns intensely, making us full of activity for God. Love, where there is nothing but pure, undefiled willingness or yieldedness, knows no sacrifice. Zeal acts in full obedience to the will of God, empowered with His mighty strength until we press beyond measure into that which pleases God. Faith laughs at impossibilities and cries, "It will be done." May God make these things immediately real before our eyes and give us these emblematic displays of inward flame.

THE NATURE OF CHRIST

The following message from Romans 5 will teach us deeper insights about God. We have been talking about receiving the life of Christ and the nature of the Son of God. We have been seeing that God's nature can be conveyed to us by the Word, and His Spirit can fill our hearts. The Word is made life as the Spirit pours it into the body. Then the body is quickened by the same nature of Jesus, with the same power over all weaknesses. In other words, an incorruptible force presses through human nature, changing it to resurrection life, eternal life, which is quickened by the Spirit and changed from one state of grace to another.

These days, many people are receiving a clear knowledge of an inward working of the power of the Spirit. It not only revives their mortal bodies but also transforms the natural body into an incorruptible power, getting the body ready for the Rapture. The divine teaching of the Lord has revealed to us the transformation that takes place in the inward life. His new nature is in the old nature, His resurrection power enlivens our lifelessness, and His divinity is seen in our humanity. Believers possess the nature of the living Christ, and with it, power over death. Do not be afraid to claim it. Claim power over sin and disease. The Christlike spirit is forming, quickening, and renewing the natural life.

The former law was of the natural man. The new law of the life of the Spirit is the manifestation of the new creation, which is *"Christ in* [us], *the hope of glory"* (Col. 1:27). Glory is a manifestation of a divine nature in the human body.

This Grace

THE BLESSINGS OF GRACE AND PEACE

Now I want to go on from that, reading from Romans: *"Therefore, having been justified by faith, we have peace with God through our Lord Jesus Christ"* (5:1). You are justified. You are being made at peace. And remember, the peace of God is different from any other peace. It *"surpasses all understanding"* (Phil. 4:7); it helps you keep your composure. You are not shaken by earthly things. It is a deep peace, created by the knowledge of a living faith, which is the living principle of the foundation of all truth. Christ is in us, the hope and the evidence of the glory (Col. 1:27).

See how rich you are in Christ: *"Through whom also we have access by faith into this grace in which we stand, and rejoice in hope of the glory of God"* (Rom. 5:2). This is perhaps the greatest of all thoughts we have reached. Faith has access through Jesus Christ into all the fullness of God. First, it was by grace that you were *"saved through faith"* (Eph. 2:8), but now another grace, a grace of access, is ours. It is a grace that will bring us into a deeper knowledge of God.

Peter calls it a *"precious faith"* (2 Pet. 1:1). It has passed through Abraham, Jesus, the Father, and the Holy Spirit. We have access, we have a right into, we have an open door to all that the Father has, all that Jesus has, and all that the Holy Spirit has. Nothing can keep us out of it. Jesus Christ is the *"Alpha and the Omega, the Beginning and the End"* (Rev. 1:8). Through Him, we may know grace, favor, and mercy, which will lift us and take us through into grace and peace: *"Grace and peace be multiplied to you in the knowledge of God and of Jesus our Lord"* (2 Pet. 1:2). Do you want grace and peace to be multiplied? You have it if you dare to believe. We have access to it; we have a right to it. The promise of the Scripture is for us:

> *As His divine power has given to us all things that pertain to life and godliness, through the knowledge of Him who called us by glory and virtue, by which have been given to us exceedingly great and precious promises, that through these you may be partakers of the divine nature.* (vv. 3–4)

We have access. We have the right to the promises and the right to all the inheritance of which He has made us heirs.

It is true that He came to us in grace. He met us in need and transformed us by His power. It is right to say that now we have within us an inheritance that is incorruptible and undefiled. It is filled with glory and virtue. We have a right to say we have the same nature as the Lord Jesus Christ.

Do we have the same nature of His flesh? Yes and no. It is true He was made in the likeness of our sinful flesh and condemned sin in the flesh (Rom. 8:3), but Christ also had a higher, spiritual order, a divine nature, a nature of love and faith.

The nature of faith is a divine nature, which was the same nature as He was spiritually. He has committed His faith to us. Human weaknesses can spoil the effectiveness of faith. Victories become uncertain, prayers lose the anointing, and the power to take hold is hindered. But God comes to us, breathes new life into us, and shows us *"we have access by faith into this grace in which we stand"* (Rom. 5:2). Now we may have a nature that has *"no variation or shadow of turning"* (James 1:17), but *"bears all things, believes all things, hopes all things, endures all things"* (1 Cor. 13:7).

An Interpretation of Tongues:

It is the law of the life of the Spirit of Christ, which is the hope, which is the glory in the hope, which is the revelation in the glory of the hope, which is filled with opening of keen perception of things above where Christ is sitting at the right hand of God, and we see jointly the Father and the Son; and so filled with purity of unmixed reality, faith rises, changes its order, lays hold and believes, dethrones, and stands fast to see the kingdom of God manifested.

A Living Faith

How can we describe this faith? It is genuine and pure. It never wavers. It is confident and sensitive to the breath of God. This faith, which is the very nature of the Son of God, comes from the Author of faith. It is holy in action, dares to believe, rests assured, and sees the mighty power of God evidenced in its workings. It is a living faith that allows us to claim all that He has for us. Faith sees *"the crooked places...made straight"* (Isa. 40:4). It sees *"the lame...leap like a deer"* (Isa. 35:6). It is not surprised when *"the blind see"* (Matt. 11:5). God has finished creation; it is forever completed by the perfect work of our Lord. We are *"complete in Him, who is the head of all principality and power"* (Col. 2:10). We are His righteousness and created for His purpose.

Romans 7 is one of those marvelous, masterpiece chapters. All of God's Word is encouraging. You can feel yourself lifted. Gravity is the only thing that causes you to remain. The Spirit lifts, the Word of incarnation moves, the life divine operates, the Spirit renews. You are being changed, made right, and made ready. Regeneration is one of the greatest words in the Scriptures. The Word of God is regenerating. Whatever you were this morning, you are never to be as you were again. Nothing will move you as much as knowing what you were so that you may become what you were not. Believe it. God's plan, purpose, and revelation is for us so that we may *"rejoice in that day and leap for joy!"* (Luke 6:23).

An Interpretation of Tongues:

The Lord's life is moving; the Lord's life is flowing. Put your spirit into the joy of the breath, and let yourself rest on the bosom of His love, to be transformed by all the Spirit life from above.

THE HOPE OF GLORY

We *"rejoice in hope of the glory of God"* (Rom. 5:2). In this study, we are laying the foundation to examine the hope of the glory of all saints. The hope of glory is that you must know where you are going. The great, mighty masterpiece of all is the great plan of the Rapture. It is the hope of glory, life divine, the peace of God, and the enrichment of the soul. It is *"poured out in our hearts by the Holy Spirit"* (v. 5).

The Holy Spirit is the manifestation of God's Son. The Holy Spirit always reveals Him to us as divine. He is so uniquely divine that He has the power to overcome. His power is pure. His power must not cease to develop. The Holy Spirit is there to create development and to help us progress in our faith as the Lord would have us to.

We are saved by His life. Now that we have received salvation, He wants to open our eyes to understand what Christ really did for us. *"In due time"* (v. 6), when there was no other to save us, when there was no hope, when the law had failed, Christ took our place, delivered us from all the powers of human weaknesses and failure, and so came to us in our sins. He reached out to us in love *"while we were still sinners"* (v. 8). At just the right moment, He died for us and delivered us from the power of the Devil, delivered us from death, delivered us from sin, delivered us from the grave, and gave us a hope of immortality through His life. We are saved by His life.

Jesus is eternal. He has the power to impart eternal gifts. He is here now; He has delivered us from the curse of the law and set us free. Who loves the Gospel as much as those who have been saved? What is the Gospel? It is *"the power of God to salvation"* (Rom. 1:16). It has the power to bring immortality and life. Through His life in us, we are delivered from all things and are being prepared for the glorious hope of the coming of the Lord. That hope causes us to sing:

Christ arose, a victor over death's domain.
He arose, forever with His saints to reign;
He arose! He arose!
Hallelujah, Christ arose!

AT ONE WITH GOD

What was it that arose? Christ's life. How did He rise? Out of death, over death victorious. Are we not *"united together in the likeness of His death"* (Rom. 6:5)? Then the only thing that can happen is that we will be seated with Him. The past is under the blood; the whole thing is finished. We also have reason to be happy because *"we have now received the reconciliation"* (Rom. 5:11). He has absolutely taken every trace of human deformity, depravity, lack of comprehension, and inactivity of faith. He has nailed them to the cross. You died with Him on the cross, and, if you will only believe you are dead with Him, you are dead indeed to sin and alive to righteousness.

The atonement, this wonderful regenerative power of God, makes us complete in His oneness. No shadow of human weakness remains. If I dare believe, I am so in alignment with God's Son that He makes me perfect. I am at one with Him. We can be without sin, without blemish, without failure, perfectly at one with Him.

Do you dare to believe it? It may not be easy for you, but I want to make it easy. In the Scriptures, we read that *"faith is the substance of things hoped for, the evidence of things not seen"* (Heb. 11:1). In every way that the Word of God speaks to you, faith lends its help. Faith stirs you. Faith says to you, "If you believe, you will receive. If you dare to believe, oneness, purity, power, and eternal fact are working through you." In Christ, we have oneness. We are perfectly covered, hidden, and lost in God's Son. He has made us whole through His blood. The Scripture tells us how it happens:

> *Therefore, just as through one man sin entered the world, and death through sin, and thus death spread to all men, because all sinned; (for until the law sin was in the world, but sin is not imputed when there is no law. Nevertheless death reigned from Adam to Moses, even over those who had not sinned according to the likeness of the transgression of Adam, who is a type of Him who was to come. But the free gift is not like the offense. For if by the one man's offense many died, much more the grace of God and the gift by the grace of the one Man, Jesus Christ, abounded to many.*
>
> (Rom. 5:12–15)

ABUNDANT BLESSINGS

Through one man's disobedience, through one man's sin, death came and reigned. Then Another came. Adam was the first man; Christ, the second. One was earthly; the other, heavenly. As sin and death reigned by one, so now the New Man, the Christ-man, will make us awake to righteousness, peace, and abounding in God. Just as death had its power through a man, life has to have its power and victory. Through the God-man, we come into a new divine order.

"I cannot understand this truth, Wigglesworth." No, brother, you never will. It is a thousand times bigger than your mind. But Christ's mind replanted in your natural order will give you a vision so that you may see what you cannot understand. What you will never understand, God thoroughly understands. He blesses you abundantly.

You know how sin was abounding, how we were held, how we were defeated, how we groaned and travailed. Has sin abounded? Now grace, now life, now the ministry abounds to us.

Friends, take a leap that you may never know what defeat is any more. This is a real divine healing chapter; this is a real ascension chapter; this is a powerful resurrection chapter. It looses you from your limitations. It moves you from your former place into a place of coveted grace. It takes your weaknesses and sins and abounds to you with atonement. It reveals to you all that Adam ever had that bound you and all that Christ ever had or will have that abounds toward you to liberate you from all that is human and bring you into all that is divine. This is the glorious liberty of the Gospel of Christ:

> *And the gift is not like that which came through the one who sinned. For the judgment which came from one offense resulted in condemnation, but the free gift which came from many offenses resulted in justification.*
>
> (Rom. 5:16)

We have been condemned and lost. How human nature destroys! We all know sin had its reign, but there is justification. God works in the lower order with His mighty higher order. He touches human weaknesses with His touch of infinite, glorious resurrection power. He transforms you:

> *For if by the one man's offense death reigned through the one, much more those who receive abundance of grace and of the gift of righteousness will reign in life through the One, Jesus Christ.* (v. 17)

How rich we are. The death life has been replaced. Now there is a righteous life. You were in death and it was the death life, but now you have received the righteous life. How much have you acquired of it? Have you received an *"abundance of grace"* (v. 17)? Your grace has run out years ago. My grace has been depleted years ago, but I realized by the revelation of the Spirit that His grace should take the place of my grace. His power should cover me where I cannot cover myself. He stands beside me when I am sure to go down. Where sin abounded, grace abounded, and His love abounded. He stretched out His hand in mercy; He never failed. He was there every time when I was sure to go down. Grace abounded. Oh, the mercy, the boundless mercy of the love of God to us!

I hope you are getting it, thriving in it, and triumphing in it. I hope you are coming to the place to see that you are a victor in it. God must give you these divine attributes of the Spirit so that you may come into like-mindedness with Him in this wonderful provision.

THE GIFT OF RIGHTEOUSNESS

Many people fail to access the divine personality of God's gift because of their fears. They know that they are imperfect. The Devil sets a tremendous trap trying to catch poor people who have made a little slip or just said the wrong thing. There has been nothing special, but the Devil tries to make it like a mountain when it is nothing more than a molehill. I like the thought that God's Son is so gracious toward us.

Beloved, where you fail in your righteousness, Jesus Christ has a gift of righteousness that replaces your righteousness. He takes away your *"filthy rags"* (Isa. 64:6) and clothes you with a new garment. He has the power to *"tame the tongue"* (James 3:8) and remove your evil thoughts. God wants to replace your righteousness with His righteousness. It is the righteousness of the Son of God. It has no corruption in it; it has no judgment in it. It is full of mercy and entreaty. It is the righteousness of the law of God's Spirit. Do you dare to accept it?

GOD IS NEAR

Being saved is a reality. There is a great deal of truth about having the peace of God. There is a great deal of knowledge in knowing that you are free, and there is a wonderful manifestation of power to keep you free. But I find Satan dethrones some of the loveliest people because he catches them at a time when they are unaware. I find these poor souls constantly being deceived by the power of Satan.

Hear this word: when Satan is the nearest, God is nearer with an abundant measure of His grace. When you feel almost defeated, He has a banner waving over you to cover you. He covers you with

His grace; He covers you with His righteousness. It is the very nature of the Son of God.

It is impossible to remain in the natural body when you experience the life of God. When you are intoxicated with the Spirit, the Spirit life flows through the avenues of your mind and the keen perception of the heart with deep pulsations. You are filled with the passion of the grace of God until you are illuminated by the power of the new wine, the wine of the kingdom. This is rapture. No natural body will be able to stand this process. It will have to leave the body, but the body will be a preserver to it until the sons of God are marvelously manifested. Sonship is a position of rightful heirship. Sons have a right to the first claiming of the will.

I would like you to realize that redemption is so perfect that it causes you to stop judging yourself. You believe that God has a righteous judgment for you. Escape from the powers of the Devil. You can have an abundance of grace, righteousness, liberty for the soul, and transformation of the mind. You can be lifted out of your earthly place into God's power and authority.

POWER TO REIGN

This holy new life, this ability to know the Son of God in your human body, is so Christlike that you come into a deep relationship with the Father, Son, and Holy Spirit. God has been showing me that Jesus meant us when He said, *"If you forgive the sins of any, they are forgiven them; if you retain the sins of any, they are retained"* (John 20:23).

This power was evidenced in the days of the first apostles. When Elymas, the sorcerer, stood in the way of the power of the Holy Spirit, Paul said to him: *"You shall be blind, not seeing the sun for a time"* (Acts 13:11). Likewise, Peter condemned Simon, who wanted to buy the power that came when the disciples laid hands on someone. Peter said to Simon: *"I see that you are poisoned by bitterness and bound by iniquity"* (Acts 8:23).

So we have to see that God through the Holy Spirit is bringing us into like-mindedness of faith. I speak this to you because I know what the Holy Spirit is bringing this church through. She has passed through many dark days of misunderstanding, but God is showing us that we have His power to defeat the powers of the Enemy. We have power to reign in this life. God has mightily justified us with abundant grace, filled us with the Holy Spirit, and given us the hope of glory. When we were helpless, Jesus Christ came and took our place. Through Adam, we all received the carnal nature, but Jesus gives a new nature. Through His work within us, grace replaces sin, righteousness replaces unrighteousness, and we move from grace to grace, toiling in the Spirit until the whole man longs for redemption.

Bless God! It is not far off; it is very near. It will not be long before there will be a shout some day. He will be here:

> *Therefore, as through one man's offense judgment came to all men, resulting in condemnation, even so through one Man's righteous act the free gift came to all men, resulting in justification of life. For as by one man's disobedience many were made sinners, so also by one Man's obedience many will be made*

righteous. Moreover the law entered that the offense might abound. But where sin abounded, grace abounded much more, so that as sin reigned in death, even so grace might reign through righteousness to eternal life through Jesus Christ our Lord. (Rom. 5:18–21)

Eternal life is resurrection. Eternal life has come into us, and as the Father is, so are we; as the Son is, so are we. This life eternal is manifested in mortal bodies so that the life of Christ will be so manifested in our mortal bodies that everything will *"be dead indeed to sin, but alive to God in Christ Jesus our Lord"* (Rom. 6:11).

We are gloriously ready. Hallelujah! Do you have eternal life, the redemption, the glorious life in the Spirit? Have you entered into it? Is it reality to you?

One day, I saw a huge magnet lowered among pieces of iron; it picked up loads of iron and carried them away. That is an earthly occurrence, but our experience is with a holy Magnet. What is in you is holy; what is in you is pure. When the Lord of righteousness will appear, who is our Life, then what is holy, what is His nature, what is His life, will go, and we will be forever with the Lord.

You have not gone yet, but you are sure to go. While we are here, comfort one another with these words: "Lord, may we please you. Father, let us become more holy; let us be more pure. Let the life of Your Son consume all mortality until there is nothing left but what is to be changed, *'in a moment, in the twinkling of an eye'* (1 Cor. 15:52)."

Do not let one thought, one action, one thing in any way interfere with the Rapture. Ask God that every moment will be a moment of purifying. Let God take you into the fullness of redemption in a wonderful way. Strive to be more holy, more separate. Desire God, the gifts of the Holy Spirit, and the graces. Earnestly follow the Beatitudes.

May God show us that divine order that will change our natures, enabling us to love as He loves, until the whole church is love. *"A new commandment I give to you, that you love one another"* (John 13:34). Breathe this holy, intense love into our hearts. Let it please You, Lord, that this bond of unity, this holy covenant with You, will be so strong that no man *"shall be able to separate us from the love of God which is in Christ Jesus our Lord"* (Rom. 8:39). May we love as God loves, and may His love take us to the peak of perfection.

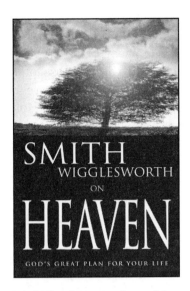

Smith Wigglesworth on Heaven
Smith Wigglesworth

Illustrating his insights with many dramatic, real-life examples, Smith Wigglesworth has a dynamic message in store for those who are looking toward the Second Coming. He explains how to prepare for your future in eternity with God while experiencing the power and joy of the Holy Spirit in the present. Discover God's plans for you in this life and what He has in store for you in heaven. You can know victorious living— now and for all eternity.

ISBN: 0-88368-954-5 • Trade • 224 pages

ш
WHITAKER
HOUSE

proclaiming the power of the Gospel through the written word
visit our website at www.whitakerhouse.com

"He who believes in Me, the works that I do he will do also; and greater works than these he will do, because I go to My Father." — John 14:12

GREATER WORKS

Experiencing God's Power

Smith Wigglesworth

Greater Works: Experiencing God's Power
Smith Wigglesworth

Smith Wigglesworth was extraordinarily used by God to see souls saved, bodies healed, and lives changed. Even in the face of death, he did not waver in his faith because he trusted the Great Physician. Your heart will be stirred as you read in Wigglesworth's own words the dramatic accounts of miraculous healings of people whom the doctors had given up as hopeless. Discover how God can enable you, too, to reach out to a hurting world and touch all who come your way with His love.

ISBN: 0-88368-584-1 • Trade • 576 pages

W
WHITAKER
HOUSE

proclaiming the power of the Gospel through the written word
visit our website at www.whitakerhouse.com

The Power of Faith
Smith Wigglesworth

Need a miracle? God has one for you.
Lack vision and purpose? Discover your God-given destiny.
Feel powerless? God wants to use you in amazing ways.

Laughing at the impossible was a way of life for Smith Wigglesworth. He trusted wholeheartedly in the words of Jesus, "Only believe." God used a simple faith to restore sight to the blind, health to the sick, even life to the dead. This same kind of miracle-working power can be yours. As you believe God, your faith will explode. Your miracle is waiting for you—dare to believe.

ISBN: 0-88368-608-2 • Trade • 544 pages

ш
WHITAKER
HOUSE

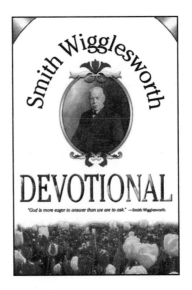

Smith Wigglesworth Devotional
Smith Wigglesworth

You are invited to journey with Smith Wigglesworth on a
year-long trip that will quench your spiritual thirst while
it radically transforms your faith. As you daily explore
these challenging insights from the Apostle of Faith, you
will connect with God's glorious power, cast out doubt,
and see impossibilities turn into realities. Your prayer
life will never be the same again when you personally
experience the joy of seeing awesome, powerful results
as you extend God's healing grace to others.

ISBN: 0-88368-574-4 • Trade • 560 pages

ພ
WHITAKER
HOUSE

proclaiming the power of the Gospel through the written word
visit our website at www.whitakerhouse.com